The
BEGINNER
WITCH'S
HANDBOOK

*Essential Spells, Folk Traditions,
and Lore for Crafting Your
Magickal Practice*

LEAH MIDDLETON

Creator of The Redheaded Witch

PAGE STREET
PUBLISHING CO.

First published in 2023 by

Page Street Publishing Co.

27 Congress Street, Suite 1511

Salem, MA 01970

www.pagestreetpublishing.com

Distributed by Macmillan, sales in Canada by The Canadian Manda Group.

27   26   25   24   23   1   2   3   4   5

ISBN-13: 978-1-64567-909-7

ISBN-10: 1-64567-909-8

Library of Congress Control Number: 2022949980

Cover and book design by Rosie Stewart for Page Street Publishing Co.

Cover illustration by Katie Beasley

Photography by Leah Middleton

Printed and bound in the United States

To all the curious spirits out there:
May this spark a magickal flame within you
that leads you down a path of spiritual nourishment
and fulfillment

Contents

Introduction • 6

Defining a Witch vs.
Cunning-Folk: A Brief
Historical Look • 10

PART 1
WALKING THE WITCH'S PATH • 14

CHAPTER 1
PAVING THE WAY • 15

Connecting to Your Spirit • 19

A Traditional Witchcraft
Practice • 20

The Witch's Ethics • 24

An Animistic Witch • 26

The Otherworld and the
Old Ones • 32

CHAPTER 2
DISCOVERING ANCESTRAL LORE AND WISDOM • 37

Uncovering the Roots • 40

Creating an Altar for
Ancestors • 51

Beginning Ancestral
Veneration • 54

Forging a New Path • 63

Connecting to Local
Community • 67

CHAPTER 3
CRAFTING YOUR MAGICKAL PRACTICE • 71

Harnessing Your Energy • 72

On the Besom, the Witch
Flies • 76

The Art of Spellcrafting • 80

The Witch's Altar • 83

Gathering the Witch's
Tools • 83

Putting the "Craft" in
Witchcraft • 86

The Witch's Apothecary
Cabinet • 89

The Witch's Calendar • 91

The Witch's Clock • 93

PART 2
THE WITCH'S ESSENTIAL SPELLS · 95

CHAPTER 4
FOR THE WITCH'S SPIRIT · 95

Cord-Cutting Candle • 96

Love Thyself Potion • 98

Opening New Opportunities Key Spell • 100

Rest Well Sleep Potion • 102

The Witch's Personal Poppet • 104

Let Me See Divination Oil • 107

Strengthen Friendship and Connection Potion • 108

The Witch's Ladder for the New Year • 110

CHAPTER 5
FOR CLEANSING · 113

Begin the Day Spell • 114

Cleanse This Space Witch's Powder • 116

Home Reset Floor Wash • 118

Clear Away Stagnancy Cauldron Brew • 120

Crafting Your Besom • 122

Home Blessing Cornbread • 124

Cleanse the Old Self Ritual • 126

CHAPTER 6
FOR PROTECTION · 129

The Witch's Bottle • 130

Ward Against Nightmares Charm Bag • 132

Ward Against Unwanted Visitors Charm Wreath • 134

Protect Me Anointing Oil • 137

Protect These Walls Candle • 138

Enchanted Ancestor Charms • 140

Hag Stone Charm • 142

CHAPTER 7
FOR HEALING · 145

A Witch's Traditional Fire Cider • 146

Heal My Heart Anointing Oil • 148

Rooted in Gratitude Ritual • 149

Support My Physical and Spiritual Heart Spell • 150

Walk in the Present Ritual • 152

Bid My Worries Away Spell • 154

Speak My Truth Charm Bag • 156

Healing Illness Charm Bag • 158

Closing Thoughts | Seeing Is Believing • *161*

Resources • *162*

Acknowledgments • *164*

About the Author • *164*

Index • *165*

INTRODUCTION

As with every spellbinding tale, a character's curiosity was sparked. Drawn to the edge of the forest, they found themselves wandering down an unknown dirt path. Along the way, they encountered enigmatic creatures, overcame daunting obstacles, and stumbled upon a vast array of magical Otherworlds. Amidst the unknown, they faced their deepest fears, illuminated by the journey they had embarked upon. Despite the trials and tribulations, they clung fiercely to hope, for this path was more than a simple journey—it was a quest to discover their own true spirit.

You could say this very tale is my own and how I find myself writing to you about witchery and magic. Growing up in the Appalachian Mountains, I always had a keen interest in my surroundings. Having moved away from the Pacific Northwest at a young age into these magical hills, I felt a pull to explore their depths. The paved road of the Blue Ridge Parkway weaving through the mountain range provided a safe haven to retreat and recover during chapters of my life in which I felt the most lost; the rigid dirt trails soothed my cracked spirit. It was within these forests that I found the calling to walk a magical path—one that I had not named for a long time. It fed my spirit and calmed my heart, and that's all that mattered.

When I met Death for the first time, a fire was lit within me to embark on a spiritual journey on which I'd find myself using *Witch* to describe my beliefs and spiritual practice. I had not experienced sudden losses before; so, when Death came abruptly into my life to claim two lives of those whom I considered family, only a year apart, I found myself opening a door with questions and demanding answers for my grief.

The keys to unlocking this door to such discoveries of my internal world and the Otherworld would be provided during an October night, just around All Hallows' Eve when the liminal space between the physical realm and Otherworld is thin. In a dream, I was visited by one of my friends who had unexpectedly passed away. It was so vivid, as if it were an old memory. The room I stood in was a bright sunroom, with wall-to-ceiling windows to my left, a white brick wall to my right. My attention was drawn to a person standing in front of me who said, "He is here," referring to my friend. I looked around, not seeing him. They said, "He's in the walls. You just have to ask." As I faced the white brick wall, I spoke the words requesting his appearance. And there he was before me. As real as he had been the week prior.

From that night on, I began a journey I won't ever come back from. Conversations of spirituality and the Otherworld had always piqued my curiosity, but this dream catapulted my spiritual journey into the world of magic. Could I communicate with spirits in the Otherworld? Could I now see them if I called their name? As a kid, I always felt I had one foot in the spiritual realm and one in the physical. When we are young, there are so many marvels in exploring the world around us. There is childlike wonder when it comes to magic, but as we grow older we also try to keep one foot on the ground. I am a believer that that magic still lives on within adults, but is drowned by the bustle of life's constant demands. If we gave ourselves the time and space to step outside and into the natural world around us, we could feel it.

Embarking on a magical journey may seem daunting at first, as one is faced with a vast realm of occult and witchcraft literature, more accessible now than ever before. But fear not, Reader, for inspiration can be found in your own ancestry and heritage, as well as in the land that surrounds you. For me, this perspective has shaped my personal practice, which I describe as a path of traditional witchcraft, rooted in the folklore and magic of my ancestors from the misty Appalachians and regions of England and Scotland. My tools are often lovingly foraged or handmade, and my incantations are inspired by the charms of old English and Scottish traditions. While I hold a deep curiosity for the lore of distant lands, I also pay homage to the spirits and legends that dwell here in North America, with one foot planted firmly in the past and the other in the present. To honor the past is to glean its wisdom and carry it forward, weaving new traditions and spells for generations to come.

When first embarking on this magical path and practicing witchery, I came across Gerald Gardner's practice of Wicca. I would be dismissive if I didn't recognize the influence Wicca had on my personal journey in the beginning, as the Wheel of the Year specifically inspired me to connect with nature's cycle in a new way. However, I never felt fulfilled with Wicca and continued following what felt right to my own spirit—forging a path of traditional witchcraft. The connection to the tales of place, the spirits that resided there, to nature's cycles and old celebrations, was all so inspiring to me. A Witch who practices the old ways of magic may be seen as more traditional, but there is no denying the power of the growing knowledge being written today in our modern world. Times change, and as they do, so do people and the knowledge that is passed along with them. We learn and we grow, creating new beliefs, traditions, and tales rich in lessons that future generations will discover. Do not dismiss the value of storytelling today, as it could be a young Witch's guidebook tomorrow.

At the root of it all, my craft and spiritual journey serves the following purposes: It nurtures my spirit, my family's spirit, and my community's spirit. What I do influences those before and after me, as well as those around me. It helps me explore my personal depths, finding the reason why I do what I do, and how I go about it. That reason is to heal and grow. To connect and to nurture. It allows me to stay accountable for myself and my actions. To finally discover who I am at my core.

And now, here you are, Reader. Taking the first step yourself down this path, following your own curiosity. Along the way you will encounter spirits, collect and craft tools, write and chant incantations, perform rites, and discover old lore of those before you—all of which will guide you to an exploration of your own spirit. You will discover an opportunity for self-reflection at the end of each chapter. We will briefly look at the history behind the definition of a Witch and what that means to you today. From there, we'll have conversations over the different spiritual beliefs that will inspire further exploration for your practice. We'll dive into the conversation around ancestry: Who they are, where they are from, and how they may be integrated into your personal practice. To end, I will share with you some personal spells and rituals that you can incorporate into your own craft.

My hope is that this book nurtures your magical journey—to inspire, create, and connect. Take my hand, and let us journey through this together, reading each other's tales and sharing spells over a cup of tea in front of the fire. By the end, you will have compiled a magical craft that nurtures your spirit and establishes a foundation for your own witchery.

-Leah

The Witch's Grimoire

The Witch is known to keep records of all their rituals, spells, and magical scripts within their grimoire. This book is valuable—a possession of powerful workings and solutions. May I suggest choosing a book to become your personal grimoire? This sacred book will be a cherished possession to record your personal findings, rites and rituals, spells, and charms. It may also include personal reflection on your thoughts, experiences with the Otherworld and spirits, and any recordings regarding your spiritual journey. This book can be as intricate or as simple as you would like. At the beginning of my practice, I was more concerned about my scrapbooking skills than recording every detail of every spell for reference, and therefore missed a lot of opportunities to collect my findings in one place because I was concerned it did not look aesthetically pleasing. Today, my grimoire is a simple brown leather book that is filled with scribbles and sketches. It is by no means a beautifully crafted grimoire as some I have seen. This shows that for every Witch, the grimoire is personal. It reflects your practice as a Witch and should be crafted in that way.

As you journey through these chapters, I will provide prompts that will beckon you to reflect upon your path and record your insights in your grimoire. Although these prompts are simply suggestions, they are designed to awaken a deeper level of understanding within you that you can ponder upon in the future. As you read on, keep your grimoire close at hand. Writing down your thoughts and observations as you grow along the Witch's path will allow you to bear witness to your own evolution. These reflections can later serve as threads of knowledge, revealing the mysteries and unanswered questions that may have eluded you before. This journey of discovery, revelation, and magic is a gift, dear Reader, and I am honored to share it with you.

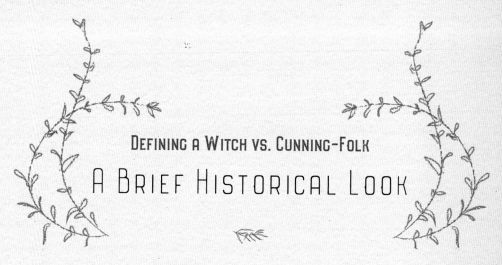

Defining a Witch vs. Cunning-Folk
A Brief Historical Look

The definition of a Witch varies with those you ask. The term is often based on cultural history and changes from region to region. Before we discuss what being a Witch means to you personally and presently, we will walk down memory lane to grasp a hold of what it was like for those who walked this path before us. British historian Ronald Hutton, who focuses on British folklore and paganism, defined a Witch by four stems: a threat to civilians; specializes in an unseen ability: inherited their magic by others; is "evil" and has a strong dislike towards humanity; and lastly, their magic could be avoided and resisted by using benevolent magic to counter the curse of the Witch. This European definition was heavily influenced by the rising fear of witchcraft in the sixteenth century. However, the concept of magic displayed in a variety of different figures outside that of a Witch, across many different cultures. For this conversation, we are discussing briefly the European history behind the term "Witch" and how the conditions of this particular term developed.

It was believed that in order to become a Witch, one must perform the rite into witchcraft. The exact traditional rite of claiming the name Witch varies by region, but there are some similarities that can be found within historic documentation from Europe and North America. A commonality of the rite performed to be granted witchery was the signing of the Devil's book, as well as denouncing one's Christian faith. An Appalachia rite of passage to becoming a Witch entailed the individual hiking to the top of the highest mountain as the sun sets. They would carry along a rifle and just as the sun would set, turn around three times while shooting off their rifle toward the Sun. This rite was to be performed for three days, as three is a sacred number among many spiritual beliefs. On the last day, the Devil would appear with his book in hand for the individual to sign with their own blood, committing themselves to the path of witchery alongside the Devil. As early as the fifteenth century, witchery was believed to be dark and feared, belonging only to those who made a pact with the Devil. Witches were granted their magical abilities through the Devil alone, and their magic would be aided by his demons, who would appear in the physical realm as animals such as cats. Witchery of any sort was to only be discussed by whisper to prevent curious minds from abandoning their own Christian faith. While the Witch was feared and powerful, others were gifted with the ability to protect their community and neighbors from any such bewitchment cast upon them.

Magic was not always believed to be the work of the Devil, but instead used in an entirely different tone. The cunning-folk were individuals residing in villages that possessed a magical knowledge inherited or taught by their community or familial elders. Their magic was a form of sympathetic magic that put action behind the superstition they believed in. For the most part, this sympathetic magic was concentrated on curing bewitchment and finding solutions for their neighbors' woes. These visits to the cunning-folk were often done in secret to avoid allegations of witchery. It was the passing of the 1563 Bill Against Conjurations, Enchantments, and Witchcrafts that endangered Witches and magical folks and practitioners, whether they were performing magic to help or to harm others. Those who were accused and found guilty of conjuring spirits or causing harm due to witchcraft were then sentenced to the death penalty. Because of this, magical folks and practitioners operated under the radar, offering their assistance behind closed doors within their homes and were deemed as solutions to bewitchment. Their remedies were often cloth bags filled with written charms and herbs to repel a Witch's magic from people or their livestock, or ointments to heal sickness or find love. These charms and ointments were not considered witchcraft, but instead the healing magic of the common folk and a gift. These remedies would vary from family and region, passed down through generations as folk magic. Medicines and charms were based on what was available and local to their bioregion, and required prayers as many cunning-folk and healers converted to the prominent Christian religion of their community. A common charm found in English regions was an enchanted cloth bag sewn into clothing to prevent misplacement or dropping on the ground, which would disassemble the charm's potent powers. Speaking daily prayers over the charm was believed to empower the charm bag and fulfill its duties while staying true to living a good life without sin. Once provided a charm for their specific intention, individuals were given instructions on how to care for their charm. Should they find that the charm did not work to their liking, or in some cases, worsened their situation, people would often accuse cunning-folk of being a Witch.

Many historical trials, specifically across Europe, were based on accusations due to personal convictions and neighbor rivalries. Those who were being accused were often an outcast of the community, somebody who was shunned for a multitude of reasons, such as an unwed woman or even a woman who knew how to read. Some witch trials involved the recording of confessions, like the famous trial of Scottish Witch Isobel Gowdie. The trial of Isobel Gowdie is an example of how historic documentation can be used as a resource for the present-day Witch to comprehend those who practiced witchcraft during the sixteenth century. In this documentation, Gowdie repeatedly recalled an encounter with the Devil and how she met the Devil on multiple occasions of celebration, along with other Witches of her coven. Along with the mention of the Devil, Isobel Gowdie's confession also provided numerous spells and charms inspired by what some suspected were local traditions and lore. The belief that Isobel Gowdie may have been a healer in her community would answer the question of how she obtained such knowledge of these charms. These trials from past Witches such as Isobel Gowdie can provide a glimpse into past rituals and practices still useful for the Witch of today.

When studying these trials and historic documentations of confessions, we must consider the extreme conditions under which many were being interrogated. Those that were accused of practicing witchcraft were often compelled to confess, even if they had not actually engaged in the magical practice, simply to put an end to the cruelty they were subjected to in prison. If they did not confess, they faced the risk of being put to death or banished from their community. However, the torture that they were subjected to in prison was so severe that it made the decision to confess seem like the only option to escape the cruelty.

Some individuals accused were falsely prosecuted due to rumors spread within their local community. The grim stories of the witch trials across Europe are disturbing and remind us of a time in which many misunderstood and felt threatened by the empowerment of the wild, free, and intelligent spirit of a Witch.

From these historical references, we see that the Witch was someone feared while the cunning-folk were the wise ones to turn to for aid. Historical documentation provides a glimpse into what a Witch was defined as generations ago, while folktales reflect the belief of the Witch while incorporating folk wisdom. These folktales can be found around the world. One that is often mentioned when speaking of Witches is the tale by the Grimm Brothers, "Hänsel and Gretel." The brother and sister are abandoned in a forest and come across a Witch. The Witch, residing deep in the woods, shares the same depiction that the Witch is an outcast of the village. The Witch invites the children inside and cooks them treats with the intention of eventually consuming them.

Here, we once again see that the Witch has ill-intentions towards humanity, including children. Though the story ends by Gretel saving Hänsel by pushing the Witch into the oven, we leave with the negative connotation of the Witch. Beyond that, we could even extend that the fairytale told to children was to protect them against strangers who welcome them into their home. But then we have the children's tale of *Strega Nona* by Tomie dePaola from 1975. In this tale, the Witch is depicted by a kind elderly woman who nurtures the world with her pasta. Neighbors visit her with the intention to find love or improve health, to which she complies, singing above her stovetop to create a magical meal to fill their desires. In this story, the Witch's image is more associated with the cunning-folk, offering a helping hand and providing a solution. We're taught that magic can be performed anywhere and is not limited to the association with the Devil. Instead, magic is found in the kitchen and shared with others. Then there are other urban legends, such as the Bell Witch within the Appalachian Mountains. This tale dates to the 1800s in Tennessee, just one state over from my hometown. The tale by Pat Fitzhugh speaks of the Bell family relocating from North Carolina to a homestead in Tennessee where activities of a spirit, who introduces itself as "the witch of Kate Batts," haunts the family. The disturbances continue to affect the Bell family, appearing as a strange figure of a dog with the head of a rabbit, whispering hymns and scriptures. Even after the passing of the father, John Bell, it's believed the Witch continued to visit the family throughout the years.

Throughout these stories, the image of a Witch is a split combination of care-taking for their local community or raising total havoc. Learning about the Witch centuries ago allows us to gain a better understanding today of how others may continue to respond to this word. While some may decide that the Witch doesn't best describe them, it is not a requirement to walk a magical path. It is entirely up to you whether the word *Witch* is one you'd like to use to describe yourself. I believe this word is shifting in tone, especially within the last few decades. The meaning has become more about a personal empow-erment and a spiritual journey rather than someone who spends their time cursing their neighbor's cattle. There is a lot of gratitude for those who walked this magical path before us. If it weren't for their stories or their grimoires, it would be more difficult today for us to learn of any old ways as well as charms, rites, and spells. It is because of the Witch generations ago that we hold so much knowledge of their ways today, and for that I am grateful.

PART 1
WALKING THE WITCH'S PATH

Chapter 1

Paving the Way

In legends and myths, the wilderness has always been an unfamiliar place. Dense forests, woodland creatures, mythical beings known and unknown, seen and unseen. The stories told of these woods are telling the fear instilled in folks' own backyards. The forest was often a place where people did not wander. It encompassed nothing good beyond abysmal creatures that live among the mossy land. The Witch walks a path leading into this wilderness, but instead of one that is well lit and paved, they wander onto the road less traveled. The *crooked path*, as many would describe it. Through an animistic lens, the Witch understands that spirit is not only within themselves but of the stones in the river and the river itself. Spirit is the stars in the sky, and the webs woven by lore. The Witch sees beyond our physical realm and often takes flight into the Otherworld accompanied by other spirits. The Witch nourishes themself in mind, body, and soul, as much as they tend to their own local gardens, community, and spirits. They are seekers of tales that surround their land, enriched with teachings and magic. They are knowers of wisdom shared only by communing with spirits. They are doers, seekers of justice during unjust times. This path leads to the magic living among the trees, soil, and the folkloric creatures. What might be beyond the hedges entering the feared forests?

Everyone has their own reasons why they decided to walk the Witch's path. To claim yourself as a Witch today has become more about personal empowerment than about casting fear among your neighbors. (Sometimes, anyway.) There are no prerequisites required to claim the title of Witch. Being a Witch is not constrained by physical abilities, gender, or race. Its definition lies in your hands—the hands which tighten together knots made of red thread and carve symbols into wood. It lives within your spirit that is thrilled by magic and lured to go against the grain of what others may deem as society's norm. In the hills of Appalachia, a practitioner of healing medicine would not have been defined as a Witch. Many would not want anything to do with that word for its negative connotation adopted by their ancestors. Their magic was rooted in their folklore and beliefs—a way of taking matters into their own hands due to little resources for health and justice. To define what makes a Witch is quite simple: an individual who practices the craft. The complexity of it comes from *how* the craft is practiced by the Witch.

Witchcraft varies from region to region, but it always has its roots in the belief of magic. Magic is the ripple in our world created by tapping into sources within and outside of ourselves. Many view witchcraft as an unseen act achievable only by those who have learned from the Devil or made pacts with other malevolent spirits. Witchcraft is so much more than that. It is the love behind a homecooked meal, spoken words of prayer before slumber, and the power behind every movement in dance. It is simple acts inspired by local superstitions. Through regional lore and that of our ancestors, we can find inspiration for a craft unique to ourselves stemmed from their old ways.

While the Witch tends to nature and wilderness, they also tend to their hearth and home. There is a universal depiction of the Witch famously brewing over their cauldron in the hearth. The hearth is an important space for the Witch. It is where they craft their magical workings to heal or to harm. Not only do we use the hearth to maintain warmth within the home, but it also symbolizes passion, creation, and power—a source of energy for our own magic. It is the heart of the home as much as it is the heart of the Witch. As we glance around, we can tell a lot about a Witch from the interior of their home. Drying herbs on the windowsill, jars filled with trinkets one may never ask about, and protection charms hung in doorways—nothing is acquired and placed by accident.

To me, the picture of the Witch within their home is a representation of what it means to create a haven within yourself as a foundation for a magical path. This exploration starts with you. Each room of the Witch's home represents a different level of their own spirit. There are rooms that may not be explored often, while others are more familiar and bring comfort. These rooms each represent the various parts that make up who you are, your unique home built out of wood and stone. To create a home within yourself is the groundwork you must do before inviting guests over for tea. Introducing ourselves to our spirit before beginning to foster relationships with other spirits establishes a footing within ourselves that we can build up from. The figurative home that you will create reflects the relationship you build with your heart, mind, body, and spirit. The Witch's path is an invitation to foster an intimate knowing of their own spirit, coming to love and appreciate their entirety, to venture through their depths, and to discover and rediscover themself time and time again. The hearth of your home was lit by the match of curiosity at the edge of this forest. Now the flame is beginning to burn and a call is coming from within the woods. It's an invitation to explore your depths and connect with your own spirit, a strength to call upon throughout the entirety of your practice.

Rite of Passage—Claiming the Witch's Path

Historically, the Witch would only be granted their magic abilities by establishing a pact with the Devil. The belief was that this was the only way to claim the Witch's path. But today, we know this isn't the case, as not every Witch incorporates some sort of symbolic Devil into their craft. There are other ways to claim the Witch's path—to commit oneself to walking toward this endeavor.

A rite of passage is most often performed when the Moon is at its fullest. This timing is quite significant to the Witch. The Moon helps illuminate the night, highlighting trails that are otherwise hidden during daylight. It is an energy that many Witches resonate with. As we have seen in confessions and trials, the Witch is making a pact to walk this path and practice their magical abilities. This does not have to necessarily be a pact with a specific spirit as seen with the Devil but can be a personal pact you make with yourself.

Some questions to consider prior to the rite of passage:
· What does becoming a Witch mean to me?
· What are some of my personal morals and values?
· In what ways are you willing to commit to this path?
· What are my personal spiritual beliefs?

Ponder these questions. Give yourself time and space to honestly answer them. Discover the root behind your desire to walk the Witch's path. Once you understand your reasoning, here is a rite of passage you can perform.

(continued)

ACTIVITY

Rite of Passage–
Claiming the Witch's Path

(CONTINUED)

TIMING: Full Moon

MATERIALS: Yourself and a candle of any color.

On the night of the Full Moon, find yourself in a quiet place.
This can be outdoors or indoors. Outdoors is a great space to
do this with the Moon illuminating the night sky, but if you're
limited to indoors that will work, too. Place the candle in front
of you and light it. As you gaze into the flame, recite the following incantation three times:

From the East to the West,

North to the South,

Above and below,

I (your name) am here to claim the path of the Witch.

I open myself to the connections of spirits who aid me along the way.

Deep within myself, I am magical.

Along this path, I seek and I find.

I am a Witch.

Keep in mind that this incantation can be adjusted. If you feel
inspired to write your own, I implore that you do so. Following
what your own spirit is called to speak for this rite of passage
will be more effective.

Connecting to Your Spirit

When I speak of our spirit, I am referring to our most authentic self—the self that is beneath the many layers acquired over time. Our spirit is the one who guides, supports, and provides the flame of passion and creation. It is the spirit that whispers when we remain silent, calling attention to our inner voice—our intuition. To create a home within ourselves is to create a safe space within our bodies. You may not have considered what creating a home within yourself may look or feel like until now. This is a valuable lesson for the Witch—to become familiar with your spirit, you must willingly tap into unfamiliar depths. To become curious and meet your spirit with utmost honesty. By gazing into the mirror and looking past the surface of who looks back at you, a door opens into our spirit. When we embark on this path of understanding magic, the key often lies in our hands to unlock the door. This door opens to a room of self-discovery that signals a domino effect, unraveling the threads woven inside us. Soon enough, you will become familiar with the ins and outs of your spirit, peeling away layer by layer to the core.

When we begin walking the Witch's path, this relationship becomes stronger the more we tend to it, adding kindling to spoken charms, knotted yarn, and moonlit rituals. Your spirit becomes a guide. It knows our heart's truest desires, highlighting the path ahead for us to follow. When moments seem bleak, it is our spirit's flame that we can call on for direction. It is the soft whisper in your ear as you approach a crossroads, gentle yet firm in knowing. Learning to open yourself and hear is a practice. It takes time to decipher between the inner voice and the one that speaks from fear. After all, this work is considered magic, as self-exploration creates a ripple effect in our lives. What may have felt true to us in the beginning may not after a nightly session of deep exploration. To unravel yourself is to find yourself, and to find yourself is to live a life that nourishes your spirit.

Picking up the mirror to place it in front of my own reflection was one of the most challenging practices during the start of my journey. I had never truly looked at myself before with the intention to peel back layers. Mirrors were something I avoided due to a lack of self-confidence, and a lingering fear of who may be looking back at me. I did not always like who I saw, let alone know who she was. Placing something in front of me that opened the door to who I am was a moment that shook my core—but, not in a way that startled me. It excited me. It was a chance to open my eyes and see who I really was after years of being told otherwise. Mirrors can be a helpful tool for this process. In folklore, mirrors are gates to the Otherworld. A mirror in front of your bed while you sleep would leave you more vulnerable to spirits traveling between the realms. A mirror can be a tool to use in rituals for meeting your familiar and traveling to the Otherworld. In my personal practice, mirrors have become a vessel for self-discovery.

A Traditional Witchcraft Practice

Traditional witchcraft is a collection of spiritual or religious practices rooted in regional folklore, beliefs, and historical documentation of witch trials. These practices are often references to the "old ways," meaning a time in pre-Christian days when the majority had an animistic view of the world with a multitude of gods and goddesses. Traditional witchcraft is both old and modern. It invites the Witch to sink their toes into the soil beneath them, reach their hands far up to the clouds, and breath in the magic around. It is wild, dirt under fingernails, and uniquely your own. "Tradition" often means historic, an antique, dating back hundreds of years. I use "tradition" here to describe the inspiration behind this particular witchcraft practice without dismissing that it is no longer present. This path references historical documentations of recorded witch trials as well as artifacts collected in museums of physical evidence of the Witch. It is inspired by regional folk medicine, songs, superstitions, lore, and harvest celebrations. There is truly no one definition of traditional witchcraft like we see within other spiritual practices. It varies from where the Witch roots their beliefs, such as the places of their ancestors and of current residence. These beliefs often reference witchcraft dating back as far as the fifteenth century across Europe, then crawl their way into the beliefs that followed in the New World. This path invites the Witch to open themselves to a world of enchantment and follow a thread that leads them along the crooked path.

It is evident that traditional witchcraft has its teeth sunk deep into the soil of place. It has grown resistant from the dark times that challenge its spirit. Upon your research of traditional witchcraft practices, you will come across a variety that are specific to region and culture.

ACTIVITY

Mirror on the Wall, Who Am I After All?

This ritual can be done periodically as you begin your self-exploration. For this ritual, you will need a mirror.

This can be done in a space that already has a mirror. Stand in front of the mirror. Close your eyes and take three deep breaths, feeling the air fill your lungs and holding it for a second before releasing. Then, open your eyes. Begin by stating the incantation three times while gazing into the mirror:

Mirror on the wall,

Who am I after all?

I see you, you see me

I am who I am meant to be.

As you open the door to the room of self-exploration, my dear friend, you will discover that the voice of your spirit grows louder as you quiet the noise of the world around you. This deepening relationship with your inner self will give rise to a newfound confidence within you. In my own journey, I found that this newfound confidence allowed me to embark on a healing journey, one that brought me face to face with parts of myself that I had long neglected. Through it all, I learned to trust the voice of my spirit, which guided me along the way. Spells, charms, incantations—these magical acts are all crafted using words that carry the power of our conviction. Your own voice can become a powerful tool in your magical practice. To uncover it, you must unravel the thread that taught you to silence it. Words are potent, and when spoken with authority, they can create shifts in our physical realm. Like a single drop of rain on a puddle, the echoes of our words can ripple throughout our world. When we nurture the truth of our spirit, our inner fire burns brightly, fueling the power of our own words. So, Reader, give yourself permission to speak with control and principle, and let the power of your words work its wonders.

Incantation to Strengthen Inner Voice

Speak this incantation during a mirror session or when you need a reminder of the power of your voice. May it strengthen your voice over time.

Hear my voice and what I have to say
The words deep within my chest
will soar up and far away.

My words loud and clear,
there is nothing left to fear.

My words are power and true,
they aid me in all that I do.

As time goes on, you will find other threads woven inside you that require unraveling and rethreading to piece together the new layer of yourself. You'll become closer to your most authentic self, removing the false layers handed to you from others. I like to think that this process is more about unveiling our most authentic self than emerging as someone else. It is not someone new, per se, but instead the someone we have always been. This practice is ongoing. There is no real end to it, as we are always unraveling and rethreading while honoring where we are presently along the way. Meeting yourself where you are currently is to honor the process of nourishing your spirit. Far too often we experience the societal and familial pressure to present ourselves a certain way. Let this be the moment you break free from that and finally meet your authentic self and the Witch within.

As someone whose practice revolves around venerating their ancestors, my personal practice is the folk beliefs of the Appalachian as well as their Scottish and English ancestors. Through this journey, I came across *Traditional Witchcraft: A Cornish Book of Ways* by Gemma Gary. Cornwall in England is a county nestled in the southwestern edge of the English island, surrounded by beaches and rolling hills. The religious practices found today in this region are like many other across Great Britain, where Christianity is the prominent religion; however, the practices of pre-Christian beliefs of Celtic* paganism can still be found through the recordings of their spiritual beliefs. (*Note: I use Celtic here as an academic umbrella term, understanding that there are distinct differences within the Irish, Welsh, English, and Scottish cultures.) The conversation of how the old ways were preserved into Christianity continues today as archaeologists and folklorists continue to uncover new findings. There is a blend of these religions that lives in Cornwall. Gemma Gary revives the witchcraft practices from Cornwall in her book *Traditional Witchcraft: A Cornish Book of Ways*. Tread through the hillsides and across the rivers, and you will find an entirely new world of witchcraft in Wales, all stemmed from the region's rich folklore and practices. Mhara Starling delightfully shares the magic of the Welsh in *Welsh Witchcraft: A Guide to the Spirits, Lore, and Magic of Wales*. These texts are a great example to showcase how being specific to place in rooting your practice will inspire your traditional witchcraft path. It is rooted in place, fed by folklore, and nourished by the physical experience of the region.

There is no way of mentioning traditional witchcraft without the mention of some individuals that developed some more structural practices underneath this umbrella term. After the repeal of the Witchcraft Act of 1735 in 1951, a movement began that birthed a new generation of practicing Witches. If you have been curious enough about witchcraft before picking up this book, you, like me, have most likely come across the practice of Wicca. Gerald Gardner spoke of his witchcraft beliefs and practices, later referred to as Wicca, in his book *Witchcraft Today* in 1954. I mention Wicca here because, although I do not adhere to the Wiccan practice, it demonstrates the movement of how witchcraft was brought into the mainstream media and the formation of Robert Cochrane's practice of Traditional Witchcraft.

Wicca had become widely popular, and from it questions emerged of witchcraft and Gardner's teachings. When we investigate Traditional Witchcraft as defined today, we find the writings of Robert Cochrane from the 1950s to '60s. Cochrane grew tired of Gardner's teachings and claimed to have practiced a much older form of witchcraft that had been passed down to him, insinuating he was a hereditary witch. Though Cochrane never wrote a book laying out his witchcraft practice like Gardner, it was the articles he had written for other interested witches that provided insight into his beliefs of an older practice. Thus, his practice of the Clan of Tubal Cain was born in the '50s. It is from this practice that we find influential rituals integrated into some traditional witchcraft practices, such as the compass round, treading the mill, and the housel. After Cochrane's death, other witches would continue expanding the definition of Modern Traditional Witchcraft, adopting some of Cochrane's teachings into their own practices while expanding on their own. Even today, we continue to see the growing definition of this term, forging its own path.

In this book, when I speak of traditional witchcraft, I am referring to the path authentically developed over time by the research of stories from your local land, personal relationships to spirits within the Otherworld, and the folklore of your ancestral spirits and the place of current residency. When it comes to forming a practice, there are so many different paths you can explore. Perhaps you are at the beginning of your personal journey as we speak over the fire. Or you've already begun but stay curious about other paths and approaches. I welcome you, regardless, to expand on the notion that, through curiosity, discovery, and experience, your magical practice will be created in a way that nourishes your spirit and connection with the divine.

THE WITCH'S ETHICS

Traditional witchcraft does not yield to a certain law while other occult practices may. Within the Wiccan practice, the Wiccan Rede is most well known. The law has had a few revisions, but most commonly can be translated to: *Do what you like so long as you harm none.* This moral code has an ongoing debate within pagan communities. The focus of this spiritual practice was on healing and bettering the self. Cursing and hexing was often discouraged to avert any unwanted harm done by the practitioner, though whether that was taken to heart by every Wiccan, I cannot speak on. Our personal experiences form our interpretations of our own moral codes. Witch trials and grimoires demonstrated that the Witch decides for themselves what actions should be taken dependent on their circumstance. Witchcraft was a way to safeguard themselves and their community from illness, harm, or theft. They believed that practicing witchcraft would offer them protection from the oppression they experienced under governing powers that held considerable control over their lives. By utilizing witchcraft, they felt empowered to resist and protect themselves against those in authority who they believed would harm them.

The Witch, the alchemist of their magic, must tread with care and consider the ethics of their craft. The power they wield comes not only from within but also from otherworldly energy sources. Before casting a spell, it is important to reflect upon one's personal ethics and intentions. Emotions can fuel us, but we must remember that magic is like a ripple in the threads that bind us together. Like the gentle touch of a finger on a spider's web, even the slightest movement can create a shift in the entire web. We are not alone on this intricate network of connections. As such, the Witch must consider the impact of their actions on others and the ripple effect it may cause within the physical realm. Take a few moments to reflect on what circumstances you feel are appropriate for such magical action.

FOR THE GRIMOIRE

To Spell or Not to Spell? That Is the Question

We see throughout history that the Witch has no fear in hexing or cursing their neighbors, as well as casting healing charms and spells for their loved ones. Reflect on the following questions in how you feel about performing witchcraft:

1. Do you believe in hexing and cursing? Why or why not?
2. When would you consider an appropriate time to hex or curse?
3. Do you believe in casting a spell or charm for someone without their permission?
4. Would you cast a spell on someone for someone else?

AN ANIMISTIC WITCH

To connect with our land is to reconnect with our wild self. An animistic view of the world naturally ties with a traditional witchcraft practice. Many practicing Witches see the world around them through an animistic lens. Every tree, fungi, flower, stone, woodland creature, and body of water that comes from this Earth has a spirit of its own. Our ancestors in pre-Christian eras shared the animistic belief due to their kinship with nature. Animism is not so much a religion, but a belief that creates a foundation for some religious convictions. British anthropologist, E.B. Tylor, wrote his studies on religion and coined the terminology *animism*. His work concluded that religions have a foundation in animistic belief. In Dr. Graham Harvey's *Animism: Respecting the Living World,* he dives deep into the role this belief plays into the study of religion, past and present. He defines animism as belief that "the world is full of persons, only some of whom are human." Over time we have become more disconnected from the natural world around us, but the Witch never forgets.

Within traditional witchcraft practices, the fluidity of structure allows mending for the practicing Witch. One of the foundations of this practice is the significance of *genii loci* meaning "spirits of place." Because traditional witchcraft is focused on working with the outdoors and communing with the spirits of the land, this is not surprising. This path naturally asks the Witch: What magic can you feel around you? What do the spirits share with you? In what ways is there an opportunity to develop a mutual relationship with the land and its stories? This resonated with my own spirit and how I found myself walking along this path. The hills breathe like a set of lungs. The rivers flow like the tears on our cheeks. To view the world through an animistic lens is seeing the world alive. That makes this human path feel a little less lonely, I think. It is our connection with the land that often inspires the development of our craft. The deeper we go into our surrounding nature, the deeper we go within ourselves. And the deeper we go within ourselves, the stronger nature around holds us.

I begin this brief conversation of spirits with folktales because I find that there is some correlation. I would dare to say that what we have retained in regard to the many spirits and magical creatures is thanks to the oral and written lore passed down. When viewing the natural world around us from an animistic point of view, we naturally may create personifications of such energies. These personifications over time may have become the inspiration behind the folktales of various spirits that blossomed and continue to be shared today. Though this book will not dive deep into all the various spirits, as there are too many to cover, it would be dismissive of me to not include the relationship of the Witch with other spirits at all. They are, in many situations, helpful allies within the Witch's journey, especially as we strengthen the relationship with our own spirit. Though our spirit is the foundation of our magical path, we may recognize that we do not have all the answers and, in turn, create a relationship with another spirit to aid us.

Flora and fauna are some of the first spirits you will encounter being local to your area. Walk into the forest and you will hear the whispers of the trees. They do speak, have you ever heard them? Perhaps exact words have not been vocally spoken to you, but the rustling of the leaves are their whispers with the wind, having conversations among themselves. Trees are some of the oldest spirits. Across many religions and cultures, trees are among the most sacred. The Rowan tree itself has many stories behind it, across Great Britain and beyond. Its spirit holds healing and strong protection properties against illness. In the Highlands of Scotland, we hear stories of the Rowan tree related to protection against bewitchment. One of the most powerful charms against the Witch was the red berries from the Rowan tree tied to red thread:

A rowan-tree and a red thread

Gars a' the witches dance to dead.

In addition, it was common in this region for cattle to be dressed in a neck collar made of Rowan tree limbs for protection against theft or illness.

Venturing out into nature is a ritual in strengthening the spiritual connection with your local flora and fauna. The trees in the woods, the streams that run through mountains, the wildflowers that bloom in spring and summer, all carry stories of their own to share. These spirits are ones that I personally connected with first along my own path, having been curious about the woods and creek behind my childhood home. There you would find me knee deep in the mud by the creek, putting together sticks and stones to form some sort of home for the faeries I wholeheartedly believed resided there. The large Weeping Willow that stood strong in our front yard became the carrier of all my secrets as I wrote them on notebook paper and buried them at the trunk, only to climb up its limbs to see the world from a different view. The Witch knows that these relationships are rich; our natural surroundings are alive, full of knowledge and friendship. The closer we are to understanding the energies of the natural elements in our communities—the trees, flowers, stones, dirt—the better we are able to understand in what ways they can be a support in our craft.

There is an acknowledged respect when it comes to connecting with the spirits of place. As with other spirits we connect with of the Otherworld, the spirits of our rivers, forests, and deserts are no different. It is a relationship built on reciprocity, to work alongside them in partnership with one another. It is not uncommon for the Witch to take a particular interest in the studies of plants as their connection deepens with their local flora. They may often become a local herbalist, a forager, a healer, or a farmer. Nature has a funny way of presenting natural solutions for wellness. Not only does the spirit of our local flora aid in magical ways, but for centuries they were used for medicinal purposes. Within the historical documentation of the Witch and cunning-folk, we see herbalism is widely used for their medicinal and magical remedies. This knowledge was most used by people who did not have access to healthcare or who turned to the nature around as a resource for their health. Some of this research was further expanded by Nicholas Culpeper, an English botanist and herbalist from the 1600s. His workings of herbal medicine and lore can be found in his book *The Complete Herbal* from 1653. By becoming familiar with the local flora within your bioregion, you can familiarize yourself with the medicinal usages of each plant.

Aside from nature spirits, we also may encounter others whose stories we've heard from childhood tales. The spirits of folklore are vast, and we often heard about them as a young child. These tales not only inspire the wonder of the Witch, but they also provide insight into the folk traditions and beliefs within a particular place when it comes to mythical creatures. From faeries to selkies, to giants and brownies, to elves and beyond, these mythical creatures roam close to our realm. Depending on the origin of tale, these spirits can be great or mischievous in nature. A tale of a brownie from the Scottish Lowlands in Bladnoch shares with us an example of this house spirit. By requesting a place to rest and food such as milk and honey, in turn the house spirit aided the family in their daily chores. In other folktales, brownies turned against the homeowners if the home was out of order and would often steal a pair of utensils, if it was misplaced. To keep the harmony among the two, offerings of honey, bread, or milk would be placed in the crevices of the home where the brownies resided.

These tales share with us how these spirits interact with humans—the good and the bad. They share how one can either protect or work alongside the spirits for help. There is so much magic and mystery that lives in these stories, all of which inspires a curiosity to learn more about them.

While there are spirits readily open for kinship, there are just as many that linger in the same woods we avoid during the fallen night. By following the thread of folklore specific to our region, we discover these spirits are prevalent in our communities. Folklore will vary with region and culture, tying together lessons to be passed on by families and neighbors, retold by generations. The stories of the spirits that live in the hills or within woods can inspire the Witch to connect spiritually with their land and with these spirits, or to warn the Witch of other cryptic beings. The stories I grew up hearing in the Appalachian Mountains vary greatly from those of the Pacific Northwest and will differ even more greatly from those told across Europe. Where there are Giants residing in the hills, there are Faefolk within the woods. These stories may carry to a neighboring region, shifting to fit into their lives. They play an important role in forming traditional ways and beliefs as it is the definition of folklore—the stories of the people.

Developing a relationship with a spirit requires time and patience. It begins with an introduction, where we learn about the nature of the relationship. Some spirits may offer guidance for a specific season of our life, and depart once their task is complete, while others may stay with us for the long term as a reliable resource. The determination of the relationship lies between us and the spirit. To build a strong connection, it is important to understand the origins and stories behind the spirit. There are many spirits around us, each offering a unique experience and connection. While one spirit may be lively with one Witch, it may be more difficult for another. Walking the Witch's path requires both an open mind and an open heart to develop spiritual connections. Along the way, there will be a spirit that we feel drawn to, and it is encouraged to explore that relationship as we navigate the crooked path.

ACTIVITY

Introductory to Your Local Spirits

Introducing ourselves to our local flora can be a start to developing relationships with spirits. Close your eyes. Where or what comes to mind first when you think about connection to nature? Is it a tree, a bed of flowers, a stream nearby? Whether it be a tree in your yard or a river on your favorite hike, consider where you feel the strongest pull. Once you have this place in mind, determine a day to go visit and introduce yourself. This is a simple introduction to begin a relationship with your local spirits. You may consider bringing an offering, such as flowers, fruits, bird seeds, or other natural elements. Be mindful of where you are leaving this offering and the wildlife around. Do not leave behind an offering that is not safe for the outdoors.

When you arrive at your destination, spend some time grounding yourself there. Then, simply introduce yourself. To inspire your introduction, here is a template you can use. Feel free to write it down and take it with you:

Hello (name of place, plant, or tree), my name is (your name). I am here today to introduce myself. We have not officially met, though we have spent some time in passing. I would love to get to know you and your energy as I begin to walk the Witch's path. Here is a little bit about me: (here you can name some personal things like where you're from, your favorite color, personal hobbies, etc.). Thank you for listening and I look forward to becoming familiar with one another.

Over time, a relationship will be built. During these moments together you will find that this place, plant, or tree will begin to welcome you when you sense a feeling of comfort and peace. The more often you visit, the stronger the bond.

Here we can also commune with our regional plants to become familiar with their medicinal and magical usages. Bring along your grimoire to record your findings. Some tools that are helpful for identifying native plants are gardening and herbal books found at your local bookstore and library, but as technology has advanced, we also have access to plant identifying apps that allow you to take a picture and identify the plant. I recommend following up with at least two resources to confirm the identity of the plant in question.

Choose one plant near you. Sit with it and close your eyes. Focus your energy on rooting into the soil beneath you. Encompass the plant into your hands without picking it from its roots. Feel the plant and remain open to receiving what comes to mind first. Does it feel gentle? Does it feel fierce? What emotions come through as you hold the plant? Any words that come to mind?

As you spend some quality time with this plant, record your experience into your grimoire to refer to. You may do this activity with other local plants around to familiarize yourself with their energy. Be mindful and remain open to what they have to say.

FOR THE GRIMOIRE

Folktales of Place

Visit your local library or inquire with other online resources to discover folktales of your residential area or any other regions that pique your interest. Among these tales, search for songs, poetry, and even children's stories. Explore the following questions in your grimoire.

1. What are some folktales that you found?
2. What are they about?
3. What spirits are prevalent in the folktales of the place?
4. What lessons do the stories offer?
5. What are your personal beliefs of these tales and spirits?

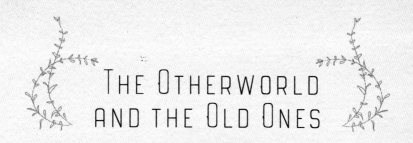

THE OTHERWORLD
AND THE OLD ONES

The Witch is known to have one foot in our physical world and another within realms outside of our own. As I mention the spiritual realms throughout this book, I refer it to as the *Otherworld*. Within the Otherworld, the Witch travels to commune with a large book of spirits—from gods and goddesses to folkloric figures mentioned before, and even with their ancestral spirits. It is within this space of the Otherworld where the Witch's spirit travels to perform rites and commune with the spiritual realm.

The belief in the Otherworld is embedded in mythology and legends across the world. Most cultures will have their own depiction of the Otherworld as well as tales of people traveling to and from these spaces. Within Irish mythology, the Otherworld is divided into various realms, with each realm populated with their gods and goddesses, spirits from folktales, and ancestors. How the Witch reached the Otherworld was by the liminal spaces found in our natural world. Like their Irish and Scottish ancestors, Appalachian folks believe that there were natural gateways to the Otherworld. One could enter the liminal space by stumbling upon it through caves in hillsides, bottoms of lakes, or deep within the woods. The Witch may also visit ancient burial grounds that were dedicated for ritual during lunar and seasonal cycles. These pockets of magical places are scattered across the world where ancient history and influential lore had taken place. But they can also be within our own backyard or local forests. Have you ever taken a walk into the woods, following the trail, and encountered a hedge forming an archway above? In the hills of Appalachia where I found myself hiking, I would often come across a trail off the one I was on that felt eerily magical; rhododendrons so vast and lush created a natural archway above as if it was a doorway into another world.

Witchcraft is not copy and paste. It is based solely on the individual's personal beliefs of the divine world beyond the physical. There is the conversation of a polytheistic belief within your witchcraft practice of following a specific pantheon of gods and goddess rooted in mythology. In my own practice, I refer to deities as the *Old Ones*, representing the divine figures whose stories are passed down through mythology and predate Christianity.

The conversation around developing a relationship with deities has been circulating around more as of late within the spiritual and occult communities. With more Witches coming into their own paths today, we see that there is no one way to honor or work with deities. Each path is unique to the Witch, and therefore each relationship with a deity will be unique and serve its own purpose. Far too often I have encountered conversations and comments from other Witches on the instructions of how to form a relationship with a deity, but the truth is that it is entirely impossible to provide a true step-by-step guide.

Before I continue any further on the conversation of deities, it is best to acknowledge that whether or not you decide to incorporate deities into your practice, it does not hinder your witchcraft practice or personal growth as a Witch. Your path may include walking alongside your ancestral spirits, plant allies, and familiars. Or, you may hold hands with a deity, or maybe even two. Perhaps it is more puzzling to the curious Witch in the beginning, as there is no doctrine to follow when it comes to deities. Alas, that is the magic in walking a path that is defined by the experiences personal to the Witch and their understanding of divinity.

The conversation around deities discusses the array of beliefs about the Old Ones. For some, there is the belief that there are many gods and goddesses within a specific cultural pantheon. For every culture and region, their gods and goddesses embody the legends of place. It is worth acknowledging that much of the information we have today about pantheons are reconstructed from what was recorded during the colonization, wars, and undertaking of regions around the world as well as the spread of religion. There is little certainty about specifics from a religion that predated Christianity, as many of our ancestors before did not record their beliefs. What we have today is pieced together from the remnants that were recorded, however the information may have been manipulated and misinterpreted based on perspective.

The Witch will find that there are several narratives when it comes to deities. For some, they include one god and goddess into their practice. This is particularly reflected in Wicca. We also see this reflected within the traditional witchcraft practice defined by Robert Cochrane's practice of the Clan of Tubal Cain as the Witch Father and Witch Mother. Then there are some who believe deities are conscious beings that once upon a time walked this Earth. Their stories share with us their life and relationships with one another, a representation of our own human journey through life and the tribulations we may encounter. For others, deities are more of an energy that we can tap into rather than conscious divine beings. Rather than communicating like we do with one another, they are connecting with the energy of the deity to call upon their virtue for assistance in spells and rituals. If we were to seek guidance in an area of our own life, such as healing, we may connect with a deity whose tales share of healing and wellness. Lastly, there is the animistic belief that the divine is around us in the natural world. That perhaps deities are symbolic representations of the world around us to personify nature. Their myths help us to define the mysteries of nature, such as the roaring winds at sea. By this belief, deities are not unreachable. They are around us in all things, available for spiritual connection by connecting to nature around us.

Upon researching the pantheons of gods and goddesses, you may come across some similarities. With wars and colonization came movement of beliefs and conforming others into their own spiritual beliefs and religion. Nevertheless, it's important to not mistake one deity for another and remove them from their cultural context. Despite some similarities that you may discover upon your research, there will be distinct differences. It is our duty to extend our research when we have a keen interest in a specific pantheon, going beyond who they are and what they correspond to, but also into their myths and legends. Where are their stories' origins? What happens within their tales? What lessons do they share with us as humans? How did the people view this god or goddess? In what unique ways can they be honored based on their legend?

It is worth briefly mentioning the representation of the Devil here due to the continuous historical reference to the relationship with the Witch. The folkloric representation of the Devil is often referenced as the "man at the crossroads." This divine figure is the one who aids the Witch in witchcraft and their magic, as well as their connection with the Otherworld. When diving into the depths of paganism, we discover the representation of a Horned God who ruled over the untamed, mysteries, and unknown within the woods. The Devil could have been an interpretation of a pagan god such as the Celtic god, Cernunnos, who was also associated with all things wild—the forests, woods, and creatures. The Witch may decide to explore this relationship further, and I implore you to do so to decipher for yourself this particular figure.

My personal journey with deities has been as clear as mud. There were seasons of my practice when I felt confident that the deity I worshiped was a conscious divine being who presented themselves during deep trance meditations. Then there were seasons when I questioned my own experiences, which led me to believe that deities were personifications of nature, an energy that I can call upon when I am needing assistance in a chapter of my life that requires additional support. What I came to terms with is that divinity presents itself in a unique way that the Witch will understand for themselves. If the Witch is open to the belief that deities are conscious beings and extend their reach to connect, then the deity may present themselves as such. I have experienced rituals in which I reached for a deity and swore that they touched me back, an energy that was present in the woods with me in the middle of the Appalachian Mountains. A spirit coming forth as I screamed out of rage and anger that lived beneath my ribcage. I felt them. I knew they were there. My eyes may not have seen them in human form, but my spirit could feel their presence. And that experience was enough for me to spiral into questioning my own belief of deities, which I continue to explore.

As a Witch, there's no right or wrong path to developing your spiritual beliefs about deities in your magical practice. It's up to us to take the time to reflect on what our personal beliefs about the divine world look like and how they resonate with us. For me, coming from a Christian background, the idea of a deity relationship initially filled me with fear due to my past experiences. However, the vastness of the divine world means there's no one definitive answer. Instead, we must look to our personal experiences to answer this question for ourselves and follow the thread of wonder. So, take some time to sit and contemplate what your spiritual beliefs about deities are and how they present themselves to you.

FOR THE GRIMOIRE

The Otherworld

Exploring your own spiritual beliefs is part of the Witch's path. Throughout your journey, you will be asked to question what resonates within your heart, to reframe what you've always known, and to question what you have not. Let's decipher for ourselves what our beliefs are about the Otherworld by reflecting on the following:

1. What do you think of when you hear Otherworld?

2. What images come to mind first?

3. Have you ever heard of the reference before? Where and in what context?

4. What does the mythology you resonate with say about the Otherworld?

Chapter 2

Discovering Ancestral Lore and Wisdom

Follow me to the home where we started. The one where we lit the hearth and began our conversation. The house that includes the various rooms representing various parts of your own spirit. Brew up a cup of tea, and listen close.

Part of creating a home within ourselves requires us to explore our own depths. It's like cleaning out the closet in an old bedroom we no longer visit anymore. As we fumble through our belongings, we dispose of the items that no longer serve us, no matter how difficult it may be to part from them. Through these remnants, you come across an old quilt. One that you took ownership of either from a beloved family member or perhaps one that was sewn just for you. If you're like me, you have one of these quilts. My mother had woven together fabrics that reminded her of me. Vibrant flower patterns paired with cream colored fabric squares with handsewn letters to spell out the phrase: *Plant smiles. Grow laughter. Harvest love.* I love this quilt and still have it laid over the back of my sofa today. It brings me great comfort.

While I see that the hearth of the home is the spirit of the Witch, I view the quilt in your hands now as a representation of all the threads that make up you. The fabrics delicately pieced together, each block representing a chapter of your life. Sewn together with threads made up of all the emotions you may have experienced thus far: love, sadness, peace, anger, joy . . . . But what you may discover, as I did myself, is that some of these blocks of fabric and threads were not created by you. That perhaps you adopted some blocks of this quilt from someone else. That these woven experiences were passed down to you, and therefore you will cover yourself in them because it feels familiar and comfortable. This, to me, is an image of the burdens and woes, as well as joys and successes, passed down to us from our family, and why our ancestral spirits can play an important role in weaving our personal practice. It's a hidden knowledge passed down, and through time had been forgotten and buried. Now, here you are with the quilt in your hands standing in a home that you are creating, reading to discover the meaning behind each block passed down to you.

The Witch acknowledges the interconnectedness of the magic that lives within them and the spirits around them. Each spiritual connection offers its own hand of enrichment along your journey. Within the line of spirits, there lives another that we cannot ignore that offers an abundance of guidance along the Witch's path: our ancestral spirits—perhaps the first spirits the Witch encounters along their journey due to their closeness in reach. For some, that is. There is a lot of value when leaning into our ancestral roots for inspiration on our magical path. It offers a unique pathway that is authentic to who we are. It introduces folk ways and traditions that the Witch decides how to fit into their own craft.

As we start unthreading and piecing together the quilt of who we are, much of the fabric we find has been looped by those before us. The question of who we derive from may arise during this self-exploration. But why would we consider integrating our ancestors when forging our magical practice? When I began my own journey, I discovered magic rich in my ancestral roots. Within these tales lived the ancestors I would never have the chance to meet: a great-grandmother who was an Appalachian midwife, an artist great uncle, and grandfathers who were hardworking farmers in the hills of Kentucky. These ancestors were just like any other common folk, trying to make their way in the world. Their families came from diverse areas around the world. As far north as the Shetland Islands off the coast of Scotland and through the Highlands, all the way down to Cornwall of England, across to the coast of Ireland, and joined by others from Poznań, Poland. Eventually, they found themselves sailing the Atlantic over to the New World where they found home within the Appalachians and Midwest. When we uncover the existence of our ancestral spirits, it opens up a path to explore the very roots of our family tree—a place where magic is waiting to be discovered. This is where we can begin to piece together the parts of our spirit that feel most at home, as we delve deeper into our past and connect with the mystical forces that have shaped our identity.

Our ancestors may not have practiced what we would consider witchery today, but instead practiced a form of magic that included crafted herbal tinctures and spoken prayers. A type of magic found only locally within their home and rooted in its lore. A magic that was simple and practical, but not any less effective. This type of magic is often referred to as our ancestors' *folk magic*. An important element is understanding the *folk*—the people. The people are the ones who shaped such magical ways. Folk magic is heavily influenced by the origins from which it was created, and inspired by the living lore, superstitions, and values of the people. This knowledge was shared and passed down because it worked. The magic continued down the line, taught from family member to member and shared among their friends and neighbors. As a practicing Witch of traditions, magic, and lore, dismissing my ancestral spirits would be impractical. It builds a foundation of an evolving personal practice rooted in the practices of people who make up much of who I am today.

Traditional witchcraft practices will vary because they are inspired by the traditions passed along by a Witch's ancestors. It is their stories and lives that are filled with a magical essence available to us if we extend our reach into the deep roots of our inner being. Our ancestral roots contain a collection of folklore that offers a profusion of guidance, which is a helping hand to the Witch at any stage in their practice. They have a keen sense of knowing and understanding about life and its lessons that is valuable—a knowledge that is shared by opening our minds and heart to a connection with the spirits of our ancestors beyond our realm. It is possible that some of these folk ways you will uncover may be integrated into your life today without ever knowing of their magical roots.

Although traditions have evolved over time, the essence of magic has persisted. As we begin the Witch's path and seek to understand ourselves, we may become curious about our familial roots. By delving into our lineage, a part of our spirit is rekindled and we discover that the magic of our forebears was influenced by where they lived, the times they experienced, and the history they lived through. These elements are integral to our ancestral spirits, and the stories they left behind keep the magic alive. By incorporating some of their practices into our practice today, we honor their spirits and invite a deeper connection with our own magical path. To uncover their stories is to ignite life back into them, opening a door for a rewarding spiritual connection within our craft.

In this next chapter we will be exploring just that—the fabrics of people that make up much of who we are today. Some may feel discouraged about where to look when starting their magical practice when much of it lives within them already. We will unveil who our ancestors are, how to discover them, and ways to honor them and integrate them into your craft. Though this is something I personally suggest and was a pivotal moment in my own practice, it is not mandatory. Each Witch has free will to decide what role their ancestors play in their craft, ranging from being the center to not being involved at all. Both are valid decisions. Your personal practice is just that—personal. Whether you decide to integrate the folk practices of your ancestors is up to you.

UNCOVERING THE ROOTS

When uncovering the roots of our ancestors, I want to take a moment to recognize that this process will look different for everyone. Individuals within the BIPOC community may not have access to accurate records due to oppression and genocide. Records of births, deaths, marriages, and more were either lost, destroyed, or never recorded. Others may have difficult relationships with their immediate family, whether they consciously decided to remove themselves, or it was decided for them. They may not have the connection to ask about a grandparent or sibling because it is unsafe for them to do so. Lastly, individuals who have been adopted or who have adopted parents may decide whether or not to seek out their biological family tree. However, that does not exclude them from incorporating their adopted family into their ancestral connection.

Regardless of the writings of your personal story, I can assure you that there are ancestors who are waiting to foster a relationship with you within the spiritual realm. They wait with open arms, regardless of if you learn their full name, birthday, and birthplace, or know nothing at all. Let this be a comfort knowing that these ancestral roots can still be discovered and the magic passed down to your spirit, despite documentation that may or may not be readily available to you. There are many different ancestral spirits we can connect with, and we will walk through an array of them you may consider venerating along the Witch's path.

The Family Tree

The family tree includes blood relatives and individuals married into family. It is those that come to the forefront when we hear the word "ancestors." It is our parents, grandmothers and grandfathers, uncles and aunts, brothers and sisters. These individuals are most common to consider when we begin the conversation around ancestors. We are directly connected to these individuals through our biological bodies, inheriting physical features and carrying onward the wisdom and grief passed down from generations embedded in our bones. It is those we had direct contact with at a young age, inheriting their language and mannerisms, while learning the ways of the world around us. Some will recall childhood memories with these ancestors, like the memories of their grandfather as he sat in his chair, the famous family dish their aunt always brought for holiday gatherings, or the quilt sewed with love by their mother.

Creating a family tree can be done in a digital space, using websites and other platforms that offer DNA discovery and have accessible online records. The accuracy of these may vary though, as once again we stumble across the harsh reality that marginalized individuals' records may have been lost or not recorded. Like a puzzle, there will be pieces that are easy to find and piece together the bigger picture, while others remain more hidden. Researching documentation such as marriage licenses, draft cards, obituaries, immigration records, and even news articles can help you find the breadcrumbs left behind by your ancestors. This information can be helpful, but there are some things to remember especially when it comes to finding ancestors who immigrated to the New World. Names were often misspelled because the record keeper did not speak the same language. In some cases, an entirely new name was created for a multitude of reasons, like starting a whole new life. Regardless of the reason, this misinformation can cause some confusion in deciphering the accuracy of piecing together our family tree. There may be an interest in participating in the submission of DNA for a starting point when it comes to retrieving records. This opens the door to recognizing not only names of ancestors, but also areas in which they resided. It's important to understand the accuracy of how these resources come to the resulted conclusion of regions presented. Most facilitations of sourcing the origins of DNA are comparing it to similar DNA around the world, like trying to find similar puzzle pieces to fit together. Though this may be insightful in areas for further ancestral research, it should not be the final destination of your investigation. Though we may discover new areas our ancestors may have lived generations ago, we can also take a look at the environment in which we grew up within our own homes. For example, if you display DNA from regions within Germany but grew up in a household with your Irish great grandmother, you may feel more connected to your Irish ancestry, having been taught more of their customs than the more distant ancestors' in Germany. When we begin to take a closer look, some information can often lead us down a rabbit-hole into the culture of our ancestral spirits. The digital world may help us discover family members, but the information is only as accurate as the source provided.

If the digital space is not an option or one you personally prefer, there are other approaches in learning about our ancestral spirits. We can inquire with the living. This opens the door to deepening relationships with our living family members, perhaps some that we may have not connected with before. It is easy to think that honoring our ancestral spirits means only those that are deceased. Our living elders also have stories that are worth learning, especially as they are still present with us. If you're still in touch with your elders, I implore you to spend quality time with them. Ask them about their childhood memories, important dates, and places they've been. Keep a notebook handy to keep this information recorded. They may even share photographs with you of other ancestors and important familial figures. Spending time with the living is fruitful when honoring our deceased. We can learn about the stories of the deceased that our living can remember and share with us.

In my personal experience, I find it quite difficult to ask questions to distant family members, as I don't have much of a relationship with them. As I write this, I have one living grandmother on my father's side who I was able to ask about her parents, who were missing from my personal family tree. This conversation led me to not only finding personal information about her own story, but also the story of her great-grandfather, James Jenkins (shortened from Jenkinson), who immigrated from Wicklow County, Ireland to Meigs County, Ohio. The story goes:

> *"James Jenkinson was a native of Wicklow County, Ireland, and was a keeper of the hounds on an English Lord's estate, and was an old bachelor when he married Amelia Martin, who was much younger than him. He did not know his age but remembered that at the time of the rebellion in Ireland, he was old enough to drive a cart. On that basis, they figured he was 100 years old when he died. At the time of the first pioneer meeting held at the Meigs County Fairground, they lined up the old people and decided that James was the oldest, but because he was not a native of America, he was ineligible for the gold-headed cane. When he was notified of the action he said that when he left the old country he swore allegiance to the King and he was a man who would not go back on his word or oath."*

> Source: Curtis Jenkinson and Jenkinson Family History

Prior to learning grandfather Jenkins' story, my husband and I took a trip overseas to Great Britain where he and his family are from. Along this trip we made a stop in Inverness, Scotland. We visited historic castles and ate traditional dishes like haggis—which, to my surprise, I quite enjoyed. As I strolled through a shoppe at a nearby castle, I came across a collection of silver pins: one fox, one rabbit, and one hound. It was one of the very few souvenirs I felt bothered to purchase as a remembrance of this trip. Before I left for the trip, I had requested information from my grandmother about her family, and upon my return to the States, she replied with this story. The mention of "keeper of the hounds" stood out to me. I recalled the silver pins I got from my recent travels and how one of them was of a hound. This story inspired me to dedicate the silver hound pin as a remembrance of my grandfather's story and my grandmother's ancestral roots, a token of loyalty and honor.

Stories like the one of my great-grandfather's can be an inspiration to how we decide to honor the deceased, and we will later discuss ancestral veneration in more depth. The living and deceased family members both carry with them a wisdom throughout their years. This is something that we cannot dismiss. Though there were undoubtedly mistakes that were made in their lifetime, there are ancestors who made healthy decisions and had good intentions to aid others within their family and community. When you begin building your family tree, you will discover this to be true. There may be an ancestor that you learn about whose spirit you feel inclined to connect with and learn more about. Regardless of how your own family tree looks, whether you are in touch with the living or know the names of the dead, the ancestral spirits are waiting for you with open arms.

Your Lineage

When you begin to create your family tree, you will start to learn more about your lineage. Your lineage is the thread that ties your family members together, leading as far back as you can go throughout history. Along this thread, you will uncover details such as birthplaces in regions that will be significant to researching the lore and traditions of your ancestors. These places will range from all over the world—some near where you live now, while others may be across the sea.

It's an invitation to peek through the window into your ancestors' world no matter how long ago they lived. Anthropological and historical research allows us to better understand the world in which our ancestors lived. There is something magical that happens in this part of ancestry discovery. Following the thread back as far as you can and discovering their ways of living paints a picture of who your ancestors were centuries ago. It inspires the Witch to reach through history and ignite old stories of the family to pass on. Memories are powerful, and when we read the tales of our ancestors' regions and history, we reawaken a part of our own spirit that holds a new kind of awareness.

How far back do we need to go? The extent of how far back we delve into our ancestry depends entirely on one's level of patience and curiosity. However, it's worth noting that this phase of the research process is time-consuming and challenging. It's not as straightforward as tracing ancestors from a few generations ago because many sources lack proper documentation or relevant information. Despite these challenges, this investigation can provide us with a broad understanding of our lineage's historical roots. It enables us to follow the thread of our ancestry into unexpected parts of the world, providing valuable insights into our ancestors' lives and whereabouts.

Crafting Your Family Tree

There are many online services that can help you build out your family tree, or you can get crafty and create one yourself. In this exercise, we'll craft a family tree that feels authentic to you that you can reference throughout your journey. Gathering this information will take some time to reassure accuracy, but oh, is it exciting with every new discovery!

To begin, start with writing your name at the top of the page along with your birthdate and birthplace, if you have this information. If you do not, don't worry—you can always use estimated dates. If you don't know your birthplace, consider somewhere you remember from your childhood that felt special, and make note of it here. From there, we're going to work our way down. Imagine a tree as you lay this out—it starts with you at the top of the tree, and we are working our way down to the roots.

Now, add your parents as an extension of you. Include any additional details you may know. We do not need to know every detail at this exact moment. From here, you will be working on each parent's side of the family. Family history may become more difficult the deeper you go. Fill in what you can, and as you go about your journey of discovering your family history, add to it. Add some personal elements to the tree, such as family crests, special locations, images and portraits, and maybe even dried flora from the places your family is from. This is yours to keep and to refer back to as more information is unveiled to you.

Ancestor Tree Reflection

As you begin to craft your family tree, consider these questions to reflect on:

1. What family member's kindred spirit do you relate to the most? How so?

2. What is a common hobby or interest that you see repeated in your family? Do you share this hobby or interest?

3. Is there any one common trait you see repeated in your family? Do you share this common trait?

4. What are you most afraid of discovering within your family tree, and in what ways can you overcome it?

5. Where are your family members mostly from? Have you ever visited, and if so, did you feel a strong connection to the land or your ancestors there?

6. What memories or stories do you have about one of your family members?

Ancestor Reflection

As you begin to piece together the lineage of your family, consider these questions:

1. What areas are you aware of that your ancestors may have resided in?

2. Do you know of any specific birthplaces, states, and countries that family members may have been from?

3. Have you ever considered traveling to these locations prior to knowing your ancestors resided there?

4. If you were to travel to one of these regions, which one would be first and why?

Discovering Heritage

As we learn about our lineage, we inherently learn about our ancestral heritage. We are introduced to where our ancestors are from and therefore can further our research into their culture. Culture is the all-encompassing term that defines traditions, holidays, lore, arts, foods, language, and beliefs of a people. This is the way of our ancestors and the way they lived their life. It is an immediate connection to the folk practices of your ancestors and where magic lives. This is especially sacred work for those within the BIPOC community—a chance to finally reclaim much of what their families lost due to continuous injustice. Everyone's process of reclaiming some part of their family's history will look different, but it can be a beautiful way to rekindle our family's spirit and the threads that make up who we are today.

There are days throughout the calendar year that call for celebration. Some of these days mark a seasonal change, a holy day, or other festivities inspired by the people. Festivities were some of the most memorable days for people, to gather with one another to celebrate with food, music, and activities. Depending on where your ancestral roots lie, people will have different names for these days of the year specific to their area. These holidays are often founded by religious practices and beliefs of areas across the world. Some cultures celebrate Saint days while others may celebrate pagan fire festivals to honor the Old Ways. In some cases, people celebrate both. What one culture may call the Winter Solstice, another may call the pagan celebration of Yule, while today we know this day as Christmas. The same goes for other important days of the year, such as the Witch's favorited Samhain, or All Hallows' Eve, now modernly known as Halloween. Though the date of the exact celebration may be the same or very similar, traditions and customs of how it's celebrated will vary. As a practicing Witch, you may decide whether to continue these customs within your own calendar year to honor the seasonal cycles of your ancestors.

In celebrations and communal gatherings, music and food take center stage, creating an aura of wonder and delight that leaves us spellbound. The melodies that echo through the land are often imbued with the history and lore of the region, creating a musical tapestry that captures the community's identity. Similarly, traditional dishes reflect the agricultural abundance of the land and the creativity of our ancestors. Passed down through generations, these recipes carry memories and stories, connecting us to our cultural heritage through traditional dishes and melodies. Perhaps you may even have a few anthems and recipes memorized by heart from past relatives?

In some cases, we may be learning about the heritage of our ancestors from afar. It may be the case that you do not currently live in the area where your ancestors are from, especially those who had immigrated to the New World. There are many reasons that our families decided to immigrate to the New World—a fresh start, a new adventure, and the promise that a better life waited for them across the sea. The information found about the customs and traditions of these far away regions may be public knowledge, but there is an element of understanding that can only be fully appreciated once we step foot into these places. Culture is vastly affected by the people's location. Communities who live near the mountains and experience harsh winters will have a different culture than those who live near the coastline. This same principle applies to reconnecting with our ancestors. If we grew up in a different country than our ancestors, our environment, experiences, and traditions will be widely different from theirs, creating unique crafts resulted as a blend of traditions and environment. From the wildflowers growing in our backyard to the fauna we encounter on our evening strolls—our local world may be different, but our blood and bones remain curious and connected distant regions of our ancestors.

When we learn about the customs of our ancestral roots, we can better grasp the traditions they kept close. In our magical practice, we may integrate some of these ways that were lost and abandoned. Their traditions are a doorway into uncovering the everyday lives of our ancestors. Our understanding of their lifestyles inspires ways to connect with their spirits and honor their lives. My ancestors are from various regions across Europe. I learn of their customs from afar to better understand what was important to my ancestors generations ago as insight into deepening a spiritual connection. However, as someone who is grasping a hold of traditions from afar, there is no better way to gain a deeper perspective than listening and conversing with folks that currently reside in these places. Refer to resources and stories by the people who currently reside in the hometowns of your ancestors for a different glimpse into the culture there. Integrating some traditions that make sense into our magical practice is an ode to our ancestral spirits with the utmost respect to those who live there today.

FOR THE GRIMOIRE

Ancestor Culture Reflection

As you begin to discover the cultures of your family, consider these questions:

1. What are some current customs and traditions of your family?

2. What are some holidays that you want to integrate into your Witch's Calendar?

3. What are some holidays to celebrate the seasonal cycles that your ancestors participated in?

4. What are some new traditions that you find interesting and why?

5. Are there any traditions you recently discovered that you would like to reconnect with?

Ancestors Within Other Communities

Ancestors extend beyond those whose names we fill in on our family tree and those under the blanket of our ancestral heritage. They are leaders, trailblazers, scholars, artists, poets, writers, historians, philosophers, activists, and beyond. Individuals who went against the grain in history and created a ripple effect are present in our daily lives. Consider the communities you are a part of outside of your family. Do you have a particular skill set or a certain profession? Who in this field is someone who has had an influence on you personally or within the industry? Perhaps consider other hobbies or interests, like the arts. Is there a particular musician who you look up to, whose lyrics lured you out of a dark chapter of your life, or whose life was devoted to making positive change in the world and sparked courage within your own spirit? When we feel disconnected from our own familial ancestors, we can look to these individuals whose lives relate to our own in some way or another. Someone with whom we'd be honored to share a coffee or glass of wine. Someone whose life was also full of lessons, and with that they gained a sense of understanding that can be offered to us through a spiritual connection. Whether they are a historic figure, local or around the world, or a leader within a field of study or a hobby, or a brilliant bright voice within the LGBTQ+ community, or even an archetype in our favorite story—their lived experience is a tale that speaks to a piece of the Witch's own spirit.

Other individuals will step into our lives who are likely to not be blood-related but whose spirit we can honor and venerate as an ancestor. If a Witch is adopted, they may decide to honor their adopted familial ancestors. Friends, elders, and family friends can also be venerated as an ancestor who had an important role in our lives. In my early 20s, I was living with my boyfriend at the time and his mother and stepfather. His stepfather ended up having an important role in my life, as he often provided me advice about speaking up for yourself. His character could be described as the jokester, someone who often made light of situations through humor despite his own struggles. There was no fear in that man's voice. When someone was being misspoken to or mistreated, his voice was often the first to speak up without a quiver. When he passed suddenly, I realized his life left a mark on mine that I'm beyond grateful for. Witnessing his courage and fearless character was a reminder to my own spirit that I deserve to be heard. Though he may not have been blood-related, his life had an impact on mine. To this day, with a locket of ashes, I celebrate his life and remind myself of the strength and courage it takes to use your voice.

There are many characters whose roles in our lives play an important part. They leave us feeling understood, seen, and heard. Their spirits relate to our own, as they've had shared experiences. Our ancestors are not just those who we grew up under the same roof with or share blood with. Far too often, if the Witch does not have information regarding their familial ancestors, they are left feeling lost with no ancestral spirits to turn to. The lives of those before us make great company regardless of relation. When we feel a disconnection from our roots, we can turn to the spirits of our community ancestors, chosen family, and others who played a significant role in our life. Their spirits extend their hand for us to grab and hold along the Witch's path.

Ancestors within Other Communities Reflection

Take this opportunity to reflect on the following prompts:

1. Do you have someone you look up to within your life or local community?

2. What other communities are you a part of?

3. What figures do you look up to within this space?

    A. Why do you look up to them?

    B. What guidance do they offer you?

CREATING AN ALTAR FOR ANCESTORS

When inviting someone over for a visit, the Witch may cleanse their space and create an atmosphere that is inviting and comfortable. The ancestor altar is similar in this way, as it's a designated physical space for spiritual connection. There are a variety of ways to construct your ancestor altar, all of which are valid and will vary depending on traditions and culture. I have found that it is helpful to have this space be an area that is easy to visit often as you go about your daily routine. The more frequently their space is tended and visited, the more awake their spirit becomes. It's like opening the door every time you stop by and say hello as if they were your next-door neighbor. The Witch may acquire a space that is more private, while others do not mind devoting a common area for their ancestral spirits. Maintaining the cleanliness of the space is considerate. Some ancestors appreciate the tidiness of their altar, while some may not mind at all. Though I have found that a weekly dusting is a polite thing to do to assure that the space is welcoming and comfortable for the company of their spirit, as well as refreshing offerings.

The ancestor altar can include an array of things. Each item is delicately placed to represent an ancestor special to the Witch and their connection. Glance across an ancestor altar, and you will find old photographs of beloved family members and past loved ones passed down or acquired from online sources. Trinkets, articles of clothing, jewelry worn, and personal items passed down from generations can also be placed here. Most commonly, you will find candles and perhaps an oil lamp as a source of light to be lit during communing. These candles can be any kind of your liking, such as votive, taper, or tealights and can be scented or unscented. The Witch will often devote a candle to their ancestors' space that is anointed with a special oil crafted for spiritual connection. You may also find something to represent life, such as a bouquet of flowers or other plant life.

Though a designated space is helpful for connection, it is not mandatory. I often find that I can connect with my ancestors even if I'm not at their altar. Their spirit is always around, and in times of need, the Witch can call upon them through spoken incantations and prayers. When building your ancestor altar, there is no wrong way to do so. The Witch will hear and know what and where to place items. Each item will have some significance. As the relationship with your ancestors deepens, items may be replaced or removed entirely. This space is your own and represents the growing connection with your ancestors. Everyone's altar will be unique to their personal spiritual connection with their ancestors. This is meant to be a beautiful, sacred space to honor those before us. Allow their spirits to speak to you and construct it together.

Constructing the Ancestor Altar

Designate a space for your ancestor altar that can be easy to tend to, whether that be a side table, a shelf, or somewhere in a common area. Clean the space with home cleaner. Then, spiritually cleanse the space with either smoke, the sound of a bell, or your own energy by meditating a white light around yourself and projecting it toward the space.

Once the space is cleansed, it is ready to be prepared. Place any items that represent your ancestors, like photographs, imagery, or other symbolism that reminds you of them. Consider personal items that belonged to them, or items that represent some of their hobbies or professions. Then, include at least one candle and dedicate the candle to your ancestors. When lit, this candle signifies that you are present with them in this space. Lastly, add a dish and a cup for food and liquid offerings.

Crafting Ancestor Connection Incense Blend

Burning incense at your ancestors' altar as you spend time with them will help raise your words and spirit to meet them in the Otherworld.

For this, you will need:

1. A pinch of dried mugwort, as mugwort is often associated with spiritual connection

2. Frankincense resin, as frankincense allows for spiritual communication

3. A pinch of dried pine needles, as pine is often associated with creating a safe environment

Burn this blend while communing with your ancestors as you speak with them at their altar.

Beginning Ancestral Veneration

For the Witch who draws inspiration from traditions and lore, the source of magic lies in the spirits of their ancestors. These ancestral spirits extend beyond our family trees and encompass the wise-folks and witches who paved the way for us today. Through their stories and grimoires, they offer us invaluable rites, spells, and charms that aid us in our magical endeavors and provide comfort and assistance when we need it most. Whether our relationship with them was forged during their lifetime or beyond, our ancestral spirits remain a source of guidance and support in both the Otherworld and the physical realm. By calling upon them, we are granted their wisdom and receive protection, healing, and other forms of aid.

The altar is the setting of the stage to begin a spiritual connection with our ancestors, an invitation to venerate their spirits in the comfort of our home by giving them a chair at the table. To *venerate* their spirit is to honor them through actions we take within the physical realm and Otherworld. There is no wrong way to venerate your ancestors, as the relationship is entirely dependent on your intimate connection with their spirit. It does not always require an articulate and bountiful ritual, but instead can be as simple as a morning conversation over coffee.

The Witch decides for themselves the intention behind venerating their ancestors. It may be to pay respect to the elders before them, a cultural tradition, or for insight and guidance of their folk ways. Regardless of the intention, our ancestors in the Otherworld are delighted to meet us. Personally within my craft, I have found that when it comes to protection and defensive magic, they are often the first to show up to our side. Other spirits within the Otherworld are more removed from us, whereas our ancestors are spirits whose blood runs through our veins. This spiritual connection is authentic to you. Venerating our ancestors is a personal practice. As the relationship is built, the Witch will learn from their ancestors how they like to be honored, but there are numerous approaches we can explore. Relationships are built on communication, trust, and love. This rapport you build with your ancestors is no different than the relationships you build today. When it comes to exploring the various ways our ancestors can be honored, I like to consider the love languages we use in other relationships.

ACTS OF SERVICE: An offering under the "acts of service" love language can translate to the service of devoting a particular skill to your ancestor, taking up a new hobby in their honor, or dedicating a daily mundane task to them, such as making the bed or sweeping the home. When spending time at their altar, you may even experience an inclination to pick up a particular hobby. There may not always be a logical reasoning behind it. Your spirit is awakening an inner knowing embedded in your bones from the whispers of your ancestors. My mother is a gifted seamstress. One year we took a knitting class together for her birthday. It was a shared experience, and I found that needle crafting came easier to me than the intricate sewing she practiced. As I sat at my ancestor altar one evening, there was a whisper that reminded me of this shared experience. When I experience these "whispers," they aren't always a voice whispering to me but instead my own spirit sending me signals to follow a particular feeling. What blossomed from this was a new way to honor the ancestors before, who used the skill of needle crafting for clothing.

I find that when we start venerating our ancestors, we in tandem begin to show an interest in similar hobbies that they themselves enjoyed. Craftsmanship like herbalism, gardening, knitting, art, cooking, music, and so much more. This skill could be something that the ancestor did during their lifetime, and perhaps a hidden talent within you, too. Try your hand at a skill or craft that your ancestors may have partaken in as a devotional act to honor their spirit. It may come as a surprise when you test your hand that you have an aptitude for it. Invite your ancestral spirits to guide you through and share this moment together. There is an inner knowing within your spirit that is inspired by them and has the potential to blossom into a new practice that is quite beautiful.

If there was an ancestral spirit who was passionate about philanthropy, you may consider devoting time toward the same cause. Look to your local charities for volunteer opportunities. Not only are you devoting your service in honor of your ancestors, but the ripple effect of your devotion creates a positive change within other communities—an act of service that will not go unnoticed.

WORDS OF AFFIRMATION: This can be written or spoken poetry, prayer, or a verbal expression of gratitude for their protection and guidance along your magical path. Regardless of whether or not you consider yourself a writer, communicating by writing them letters or within a devoted journal can be easier for those who struggle to speak what is on their heart. I find this method to work well when sharing my woes with my ancestors. Speaking to them out loud becomes difficult, but I find the words come better when I am writing fluidly without worry if anyone outside will hear me. If writing feels more daunting, speaking to them is just as effective. Imagine they are with you in the room—because spiritually they are. Take this opportunity to express gratitude. Our ancestral spirits do work in the Otherworld that we may not know about and come to our defenses to protect us from harmful energies or physical situations. They remove situations that do not align with our Witch's journey to guide us on the path that is meant for us, no matter how difficult it may be. When seeking protection, our ancestors are often the first to come to our side and fend off ill-intentioned people from our lives. Verbal gratitude roots us in an appreciation for their spiritual guidance in our practice. Words hold so much power when spoken from the heart. Share with them some of your favorite writings, like poems, songs, fairy tales, lore, or any other literature that is special to you. Like some of our ancestral spirits in their living days, exchanging personal and fable stories connects us together.

QUALITY TIME: This love language is simple, yet one of the most important and quite valuable. Spending time at their altar space with them on a frequent basis to get to know them reaffirms the bond between your spirit and theirs. Allow their voice to be heard in these moments. Simply taking a few quiet moments to sense the spirits at their altar, even when you're not performing any actions, sends a clear message that you acknowledge their presence. It's like a quick hug or hello that reassures them that they are not forgotten as you go about your day. A morning ritual I have for my own veneration practice is drinking my first coffee of the day with them. I will pour some of my coffee into their cup at their altar. This approach is one of the simplest, but it has been the most effective in venerating their spirit.

GIFT-GIVING: Gifts are a common offering to spirits and come in many different forms, whether handcrafted, purchased, or even cooked. Despite the value of the item, your ancestors do not require glamorous gifts to feel your appreciation and love—unless you are venerating an ancestor who enjoys the luxuries of life. A gift can simply be a flower picked on your afternoon walk in the park. It can be something you made by hand, like a painting or needlework. The intention behind the gift-giving is what matters, not the price tag. In some cultures, there are traditional items that hold a meaningful connection to their home. Placing a gift at their altar can be a sign of appreciation for their guidance.

With these love languages in mind, the Witch will learn in what ways their ancestors' spirits respond and which ones they appreciate most, as each spirit will have their own preferences. Learning about our ancestors as individuals in their lifetime allows us to better understand the unique way to honor their life. When this information cannot be obtained, the Witch may inquire with them through divination or spirit flight. Each ancestral spirit will have their own preferences, but we can attempt each way that speaks to our intuition to learn their unique love language. There are other ways to venerate our ancestral spirits. The goal is to connect with them on a deep level, and therefore, approaching the connection by placing ourselves in their shoes is just another way to reach them. In this way, we can consider the food they ate, the place they lived, the language they spoke, and even the stories they read.

FOOD AND BEVERAGES OFFERINGS: Food and beverages are another common offering used to venerate our ancestors. They are often the center of festivities and celebrations. As we nourish our own bodies, prepping and cooking a traditional dish as an offering can also nourish the spirit of our ancestors. The kitchen is a space of community and love. There we can honor our ancestors by prepping their favorite meal or a traditional dish, leaving a plate at the altar for up to three days to feed their spirit. If you're concerned about pets or children coming into contact with the offering, you may conceal it how you see necessary, and place it out of reach. Beverages can also be an option for an offering. Some ancestors celebrate with spirits like whiskey or wine. If the ancestors are ones who practiced a religion in which wine was used in such a way, they may appreciate a glass themselves. It is always polite to consider the relationship they had with such spirits prior to offering. If an ancestor had struggled with the illness of alcohol addiction, it may be considered inappropriate to leave them an offering of such. The same goes for their history with food. If there was any ancestral spirit whose relationship with food might have been morphed from fear of famine and lack of resources, we may offer our leftovers for their enjoyment at the altar to feed their spirit. We may also consider sharing a meal with them, as supper was often a shared time of day with families. Nevertheless, a beverage or treat of some kind is often enjoyed by ancestors. When in doubt or unsure, a glass of clean water set at their altar will do just fine before learning what other beverage and food offerings they'd enjoy. Water allows the spirit to move through more freely and is a helpful element for the spirit to travel between realms.

VISITING ANCESTORS' HOMELAND: Though not everyone has the means to visit the land where their ancestors are from, visiting their homeland is one of the ways to honor their spirit. By visiting their hometowns, states, or even the country, there is a connection we have with these areas that can be felt within our body. We get to witness the landscapes that were so familiar to them. When I started to develop my ancestral veneration practice, I took it upon myself to begin visiting the places I found in my research, far and close. I implore that if the resources are available, do take a trip to one of your ancestors' homeplaces. When we get the opportunity to experience these places rather than just read about them, we see an accurate depiction of the place and people, firsthand. There is an invisible string that leads you there, leaving a feeling of connection waiting to be nourished.

LEARNING THEIR LANGUAGE: When communicating with ancestral spirits far in our lineage, it is not uncommon to discover a language that is different from ours today. Language is one of the many things that is influenced by history. Between colonization and wars, the language of the people will shift and adapt to that of their oppressors. There are endangered languages found across the world. Some are so ancient to uncover, as they have not been used or spoken in centuries. Learning the language of our distant ancestral spirits can be a contribution to their old ways. If the Witch is honoring ancestors from a different region, learning the language of the people is one of the ways to pay respect to their origins and reduce its diminishment. Not only will it help when communicating with our ancestral spirits who resided in lands far from our own, but it also allows us to reclaim part of that history back into our family. There will be literature of heritage and cultural traditions written in these languages that are not translated into the current language we may speak today. It is not required to learn these languages when communicating with our ancestral spirits, as I believe that even without spoken words, they can still read what lives in our spirit. But taking the time to learn to speak, write, and read the languages of our ancestors can lead us to treasured resources of sacred texts specific to our ancestors' lands.

STUDIES OF FOLKLORE: There is a web intertwined within stories passed on that weaves us together. There is magic to be uncovered within the ancestral lore. It allows us to better understand the stories of our ancestors for insight into their lives. The folklore of our ancestors resides deep within the forests of their homes. It's in the ivy that crawls up the distressed brick buildings whose walls hear of the superstitions and mythical creatures told by candlelight. In these stories we hear our ancestors. Their fears, their beliefs, their values, and their life lessons. Each tale varies from region to region. The stories told at the bottom of the mountain will differ from the ones told by the seaside cliffs; each land has its own beings that roam their villages to be feared, to be sought, and to be worshipped. In the stories, the Witch can discover new ways to connect with their ancestral spirits. For instance, a tale of a local flora of Yarrow that lives in the depths of English gardens may find itself across the sea in our own backyard—a connection between plant, tale, and the people before us who shared its magical properties of healing and protection. Or the Faefolk whose tales reached across Great Britain, each region sharing their individual beliefs. These otherworldly beings were silent dwellers who lived underground, waiting to either grant wishes of the people or to take away their luck. The faeries could grant the people their wishes. Though it would appear this was a blessing, the gifts from the faeries would include inevitable bad fortune that would eventually find them. Thus, stories and tales like these shine light on the superstitions passed along and the ways in which ancestors could protect themselves. For instance, iron was used to protect against faeries. Iron is a powerful protection metal and can be used in any form to protect against misfortune casted by the faery, such as a knife or nail. Often one would store the knife or nail within a pocket while traveling home in the night to avoid being picked away by the faeries. By reading the folktales from regions of our ancestors, we learn about their rooted beliefs and folk ways.

Our ancestors lived full lives like we are now. The discovery of their personal stories sets the tone for who they were in their lifetime. It can be eye-opening to hear about their life. We paint the picture of their faces, their clothes, their favorites dishes, the songs they listened to, and the tales told around the bonfire. When we share the stories of passed loved ones and the wise before us, we are bringing life back into their spirit from the Otherworld. Spoken word, healing tinctures, sacred herbs, and verses from books and grimoires encompass magic performed by ancestors to be passed unto you. Their spirit moves through you as you integrate these beliefs and practices into your own witchcraft. Within these untold narratives, the discovery of antiquity and tradition leads us down an authentic magical path.

Summoning an Ancestor

There is an ancestor beyond the veil that is awaiting your invitation. This ancestor can be referred to as an ancestral guide. Whether they are blood-related or within our community, they offer protection, guidance, and knowledge—an aid that is beneficial for the Witch along their ways.

If you have a specific ancestor in mind to summon, you may perform this ritual:

Acquire a portrait of your chosen ancestor along with a piece of paper with their personal details that you know, starting with their name. Add their birthplace and birthday if you know it. Place this piece of paper next to their portrait.

Gather personal items of this ancestor if you have them. Items can include things like an article of clothing, a lighter they owned, or a piece of jewelry—anything that was in their possession.

Consider an offering for their spirit. Make them a plate of their favorite food, offer them candies or other treats they enjoyed.

Arrange the items you've gathered and a candle in a way that resonates with you, creating a mini altar for their spirit. Place a small glass of water beside the altar for their spirit.

Sit before the mini altar space you created. Spend a few moments here, grounding your spirit by getting in a comfortable position and visualizing yourself rooted in the ground beneath you. When you feel ready, light the candle. Begin shifting your weight in a circular motion to enter a trance-like state, keeping your eyes on the candle's flame. As you enter a trance-like state, chant the incantation:

My beloved ancestor, (state name),
I invite your spirit into my space,
Encompass me with love in this place.
I ask your spirit for this chance
to meet you in this trance.

Allow space for the ancestor's spirit to come forth, trusting your intuition in this moment. Do you sense a presence nearby? Do words or feelings arise without explanation? In this moment you may not feel anything, but continue practicing this ritual until your ancestor comes forth.

Once the ritual is complete, give thanks to the ancestor for sharing this moment with you, whether they shared anything or not. Blow out the candles and return their belongings to the ancestor altar.

If you do not have a specific ancestor in mind to summon, you may perform this ritual with the candle and water only, replacing the incantation with:

My beloved ancestors of unknown,
I invite your spirit into my space,
Encompass me with love in this place.
I ask your spirit for this chance
to meet you in this trance.

Ancestral Spirit Reflection

Take this opportunity to reflect on the following prompts after you have performed the ritual:

1. Did you feel a particular presence? If so, describe it as best you can.

2. Did a particular thought or feeling arise? If so, describe it as best you can.

3. Did any imagery or visualizations within the mind arise? If so, describe them.

If you performed the ritual and did not have any of the above occur, do not feel discouraged. There are a few reasons why this may happen. The ancestral spirit may not be ready to present themselves, as it is a new relationship. Consistently extending your reach to connect is key to opening the door for them to communicate. Perhaps they may respond a few days later within your dreams, during meditations, or in another way. Keep an open mind during this time and record any dreams, meditations, or experiences that follow. As you build this spiritual connection, you will learn of ways this ancestor communicates with you. This can be a variety of ways, such as dreams, visuals during ritual, an inkling of emotion, random words or phrases that come to mind, or other divination methods such as sending specific animals. This unique way of communicating with one another is developed over time as you continue communing with them.

FORGING A NEW PATH

It may be easier to ignore the rotted roots of our familial tree. But if nature taught us anything, it's that eventually the rot will become detrimental to the tree's overall well-being. For some individuals, the conversation surrounding family can be a weight on the shoulders. It is undoubtedly true that when researching your lineage, you will come across what I consider to be troubled ancestors. These are the ancestors whose shadows linger in our family stories. Our ancestors were not immune or exempt from life's lessons. They experienced hardship and trauma and made mistakes in some chapters of their lives. These may be family secrets that are currently covered by a thick layer of moss. A sort of shameful or uncomfortable truth. There will be moments in our lives when we mirror similar mannerisms and behaviors adopted unconsciously from our ancestors, the good and the ugly. They will play out in their unique way right before our eyes in our everyday life—in relationships with others as well as with ourselves. However difficult it may seem, it is an opportunity to take these old wounds and pour liquid honey over them for healing. Every Witch will uncover unnerving beliefs, behaviors, and experiences within their own tree. Some of these may no longer serve our pathway. The awareness of our ancestors' mistakes from the past, however, allows us to address them how we see fit to support a healthier familial tree. But it is clear that certain behaviors and actions are not forgivable from ancestors who caused harm and danger to other people. Healing does not always equate to forgiving. It is a personal journey that only you will define for yourself. In some cases, this undertaking of deconstructing woven fabric from our ancestral spirits can be the rethreading of who you are.

I am not a psychologist and would recommend extending your resources to the scientific research of how our bodies are intertwined genetically and the adoption of trauma from earlier family members. All I can speak on is my own experience and how I discovered how ancestral trauma plays a role in my life. As I started my own healing journey, I unthreaded a particular story around relationships that was woven deep within my unconscious mind. The instability and fear of relationships was a hidden truth I found within the crevices of my family. It was a discovery I would have in my mid-20s through my efforts in therapy. Why, despite having a supportive, loving partner, did I find myself avoiding the acceptance of love? Why was I adamant that our partnership would end in shambles when we had overcome obstacle after obstacle, showing up more as our true selves than the time before? It was a fear embedded in my bones from the experiences of my family generations ago. It was like playing a script that was written for someone else, but I had it memorized. So, why wouldn't I also play the role? This fear was engraved in my mind even though my heart knew better. It played out before me as self-sabotaging behaviors and anxiety disorders. What I found was that the role I was playing was that of a grandmother who had experienced heartbreak within her own relationship. One that was filled with deceit and dishonesty. One that left her to raise the children they had together alone so that he could start a new life. The heartbreak and grief this grandmother had experienced trickled down into her daughters and sons. I found that the coping mechanisms I adopted for myself were to protect my heart from the same story my grandmother had lived. This anguish may not have appeared to be something challenging enough for future generations to experience the effects, but trauma is such an overarching term that encompasses any experience that leaves us feeling less than who we are. Though I do believe our spirits are intertwined with our ancestors, I can acknowledge that our physical bodies could be, too.

When we are overcoming a trauma so deep, professional guidance from someone within the mental health field can be the light at the end of the tunnel. I like to think that ancestral veneration works well in partnership with other sources like therapy for emotional well-being. Therapy is not always accessible due to available resources. There are some organizations that offer financial assistance, such as the Open Path Collective (openpathcollective.org). This allows individuals who do not have insurance or require a sliding scale in pricing to connect with a local therapist. Attending therapy for the last several years has done wonders for my spirit, mind, body, and heart. I only share that to inspire anyone who has considered it to look further if it is a path for your own healing journey.

The New World was founded on pain, and that is still very prevalent today. While some ancestors participated in the genocide and enslavement of others, there were families on the receiving end who faced these calamities. These experiences are defined as *ancestral trauma*—an experience that shifts the chemicals within the body and can be passed down the family tree. Trauma has been widely spoken about for the last decade as further research reveals the effects it has on the physical body and psyche. It is not only the horrific experiences such as war, genocide, and enslavement that our ancestors experienced—it extends to other events that leave a mark on our spirit. Trauma is both an individual experience and an experience for a generation or group of people. This is referred to as *historical trauma*. The terminology to describe the lived experiences of a group of people and the major events they experience was coined by Dr. Maria Yellow Horse Braveheart, a psychologist, president of the Takini Institute, and director of Native American and Disparities Research in the Center for Rural and Community Behavioral Health at the University of New Mexico. Her extensive research focuses on the effects of cross-cultural mental health and historical trauma, such as the colonization of the New World and the Holocaust. Historical trauma shows us that somewhere along the line, we had an ancestor who was affected by the world's major events. They were either individuals who took part in the tragedies or were on the receiving end of them. We may even have a blend of ancestors who experienced both. There is healing work to be done for both sides—accountability and responsibility as well as healing and nourishment.

When we come across a troubled ancestor, it is up to us to decipher how we want to approach them, if at all. Like with the living, boundary setting is essential to protecting your healing and peace. When we are venerating our ancestors and we come across these troubled ones, we are allowed to establish a boundary like restrictions from entering your sacred space. These ancestors whose beliefs do not align with ours, those who participated in tragedies, and overall unkind people may not be the family we would want to venerate for our practice. For example, if an ancestor gambled away all the family's money and brought unwanted debts, they may not be the best to ask for assistance with wealth and prosperity. When addressing our ancestors, we can exclude the ones whose lives caused more pain than good. Their behavior is not something we would want to learn from. Instead, we can take this opportunity to heal the rotted roots, but not before addressing and learning from their mistakes.

Within the spiritual community, there's been a swirl of conversation around *spiritual bypassing* regarding the topic of becoming self-aware. Life is messy. Humans are too. Look to the Moon and you will see that even our favorite friend in the night sky has both an illuminated and shadow self. Spiritual bypassing is a term coined by John Welwood, a psychologist and spiritualist who recognized this dismissive behavior happening within spiritual communities. He described it as, "to use spiritual ideas and practices to sidestep or avoid facing unresolved emotional issues, psychological wounds, and unfinished developmental tasks." It is much easier to sweep dirt under the rug and forget about it. It takes strength and self-awareness to look at the source of the dirt. That is part of the healing journey. Some would rather ignore this process, whether they are in denial of the unpleasantry of trauma or just aren't sure of where to begin. To deny one's struggles is to deny their humanness. Every person, whether they speak on it or not, have experienced some form of hardship.

There are people who may no longer be directly in contact with their biological family. In these cases, those who have decided to form their own path different than their families' may be disconnected from parts of their ancestral roots, either by choice or circumstance. This can be detrimental when it comes to venerating blood relatives with whom we do not have any connection. There is a weight on the chest that may require time to grieve the idea of what family means and who all that entails. Grief is often related to the deceased, but it can also relate to the living. Sometimes we grieve for the "ideal" family we see in media or by witnessing our own friends and neighbors' healthy familial relationships. Not everyone is granted the gift of a family that supports them unconditionally. It is a harsh reality, and there is a grieving process that takes place. But as we spoke before in regards to who we consider our ancestors, we know that they extend beyond those whose relationships may be strained.

There is as much pain as there is good when reading the stories of our ancestors. The work of self-exploration allows us to look in the mirror within ourselves and even within our own family. Our ancestors lived in a much different world than we do today. Their resources and societal standards were different, and they lived through traumatic major events throughout history. We may never fully understand their actions or decisions, no matter how unfair or even cruel they were. Educating ourselves on the years they lived in can provide some insight though. If our ancestral spirits resided in the New World within the 1950s, they were most likely abiding by the societal standards of domestic households and gender norms; the years that followed after World War II resulted in our elders experiencing PTSD. As we learn about our ancestors and their lives, we may not entirely grasp a hold of their reality. No matter how badly we want to place our feet in their shoes, it is physically impossible to ever really know.

Much of what they experienced moved up from the roots and into the branches of the tree. Now, it is up to the Witch to decide whether to do the work of cutting the limbs to leave room for healthier leaves. As we begin to unthread what has been previously woven for us, we will find deeply rooted threads that no longer serve us. It's an unwanted lingering anger resting heavy in our chest. It's a tension within the body that alerts us even when there is peace. It is unkind words fed in our minds throughout the day when there are no worries. The hardships of our ancestors can sometimes be the answer to unanswered questions of our own mannerisms. What burdens have we taken on that perhaps belonged to a previous family member?

This work is part of the rethreading of who we are that the Witch undertakes in their journey. The unthreading of this fabric requires us to reveal hidden truths that were kept quiet for generations. Difficult? Absolutely. Rewarding? Also, yes. But this exertion leads to the formation of new fabrics for a new path ahead and one that you can proudly create for yourself.

Connecting to Local Community

While there is great value in connecting to our ancestral spirits, there is just as much magic in connecting to the people within our local community. Though I have extended my personal research of my ancestors across Europe, I grew my roots within the Appalachian hills. It is within these mountain communities that I found my home, and the people here are the ones who became family. Our local communities hold so much encouragement for us. There are individuals locally who share a similar story and path. While we may romanticize the abroad connection of our ancestral spirits, there is no doubt that the relationships we foster with our local communities are just as fruitful. As we have seen in the folklore of the Witch, they are active members of their communities. They tended their neighbors' needs, magically and medicinally, and provided an ear to listen and a warm meal made with intention.

Let this be inspiration to seek individuals whose stories resonate with yours within your neighborhoods. By connecting with our local community, we open the door to a special kind of connection that aids the Witch on their path. A lot of healing can be done with our neighbors. You never know, you may be the one to form a coven . . .

Addressing a Troubled Ancestor

Prior to this ritual, consider the boundaries you would like to create with your troubled ancestors. How do you consider them to be troubled? What would they have done in their lifetime to where you would not want to share space with them?

Whether we know the names of a troubled ancestor or not, we can use this ritual to acknowledge their existence once upon a time and establish boundaries.

Once we have gathered our thoughts and what boundaries we are setting in place, sit at your ancestor altar on the Full Moon. If you do not have one, create a space at your altar with imagery, belongings, or other representations of your ancestors. If you have information about a specific troubled ancestor you would like to address, gather the materials and information here. Write their name down on a piece of paper along with any other information. Again, this is not needed in order to move forward with this ritual.

As you sit at the altar, light a white candle to represent purification. Once the candle is lit, focus on grounding your energy in the present moment.

When you feel ready, state the incantation:

Beloved wise and well, Ancestors,
I call upon you, and invite you into my space
To help me address the wounded and what they faced.
To the troubled ancestor, I say to thee
These boundaries I set to be:
(State your boundaries firmly here).

Beyond this, I hope you hear
that though you are not welcome near,
the healing I do is for us
You may disagree, but please do trust
A new path is created before me
Healing the wounds that I see.

I ask that you respect these ways
Today and tomorrow, all of my days.
Beloved wise and well, Ancestors,
I thank you for your protection from the troubled
that lie buried within the tree,
Continue to show and guide me,
To a better way to be.

Allow a few moments for any messages from your ancestral spirits to come forth; they may show you imagery, feelings, or words at this time. Some guidance may be provided during this ritual of how to approach a troubled ancestor if they are quite stubborn.

To end the ritual, blow out the candle and express gratitude for the ancestral spirits.

CHAPTER 3
CRAFTING YOUR MAGICKAL PRACTICE

Throughout this book, we dove into the historical and personal meaning behind being a Witch, taking a walk across Europe into the New World and within ourselves. We dove into our depths and uncovered the reason behind the spark that lives within our spirit. The foundation has been laid before us in many ways, from self-discovery and reclaiming of our personal power, to the stories of our ancestral spirits, and to the land of our backyard and the spirits met within the Otherworld. Now, we take the staff gifted to us by the woods, our cauldrons, and walk under the moonlit night.

Witchcraft is the intertwining of all things the Witch finds themselves putting into practice—spirit communing, herbal knowledge, development of intuition, and beyond. Witchcraft encompasses all the rites, rituals, and magic of the Witch. Witchcraft is as much reviewing the old grimoires from the Witches that paved the way as it is working their charms and spells. The curious Witch may wonder where the crooked path will lead them, but it is the enticing magic that lives beneath the surface that pulls you in. To unveil the magic living within the wilderness. What knowledge are we opening ourselves to? What is beyond that calls our spirit to unearth and experience? This practice asks us to place ourselves in the liminal space and create ripples in the water of our world that meets our desires so close to our own spirit. To yield powers of energies around and within ourselves to create *change*.

Here I will walk you through crafting a magical practice, but ultimately the one that you create requires one thing—that it *works for you*. If we have learned anything thus far, it is that the Witch's practice is constructed to help them. That is why many practices vary—every Witch is unique in their approach. All of the provided information I'll share is inspiration for getting started or for incorporating something new into a practice you already have created. This book is perhaps your first step onto the Witch's path, or perhaps it is reigniting the flame underneath your cauldron that has built a bit of dust. However you see this book and what lies ahead now is entirely up to you to experiment with and attempt for yourself. Omit things, replace them, test them. This is *your* magical practice, and nobody has agency over how you build it.

Harnessing Your Energy

Becoming familiar with your own energy helps decipher it from other energies that you will encounter. It is the main source to tap into when projecting and manipulating energy within your craft. There are other sources the Witch may derive energy from when casting a spell. There is the energy of the elements, spirits, plants, deities, and ancestors. How you experience your energy may be quite different from other Witches. Some experience a sensation through their body, while others may see with their Witch's eye a swirling cloud within the center of their body. With practice, you will strengthen your ability to sense and control your energy to charge and cast spells.

Grounding is a practice that allows you to take root in your own energy. Throughout the day, our energy disperses based on what is required of us—a job, a family to tend to, gatherings with friends; all of these require energy from us. It is easy to leave behind pockets of our energy in these places, leaving us tired and weary after a long day. To ground our energy helps us to recall this energy and restore what we've left behind. It's replenishing and helps center our mind as much as our physical body.

There are a few methods one can use to practice grounding. A personal favorite is to seek a safe space outdoors. This can be in your own backyard, your favorite park, or even a rock on your favorite hiking trail. Perhaps it is a specific tree you feel inclined to lean on somewhere outdoors. Living in the Appalachians, I was spoiled by having access to the Blue Ridge Parkway, a road leading from Georgia all the way up to Maryland. This road has access to many little trails leading into the woods. When seeking solace, often I would hop in the car, drive a few miles on this highway, and pull off to one of the trails to explore. My spirit always felt at peace as I trekked up the trail, finding reconciliation on a nearby rock or stump. Finding a space that allows you to feel safe will be beneficial with grounding practices, especially those that are outdoors to reconnect with the natural world.

Take Root

Take yourself to a space that feels safe to you, whether that be indoors or outdoors. Sit or lay down here, depending on what position feels most comfortable. Take a few breaths, tuning in to your chest as you do so. At this time, it is completely normal for your mind to wander. Instead of resisting, allow the thoughts to come, letting them go without lingering for too long. Focus your attention on your body, starting from the crown of your head working your way down to your toes. Take note of any muscles that feel tense, allowing yourself to release the tension.

From here, direct your attention to the space between where your body is touching and the surface beneath you. Tune into this space for a few breaths. With the Witch's eye, visualize your body creating roots to the ground beneath. Focus on being present in this moment. Feel into it with your roots growing deeper below. To remain focused, here is an incantation you can recite in your mind:

My body take root here,
My mind steady and clear.

Learning to ground your energy preserves your energy for any spell working you decide to cast and allows you to step into a meditative state. Not only is it beneficial for magical workings, but it is a form of nourishment for your spirit. Our energy is sacred to protect. Take note of what may drain your energy throughout the day, whether that is a specific place, person, or activity. The act of setting boundaries is of great importance when preserving your energy. Every day, we encounter opportunities that can either drain or nourish our spirit.

(continued)

Take Root

When we discover what depletes our energy, we can establish these boundaries for ourselves and others to protect us from misplacing our energy. This will take some time and is often discovered along the Witch's path. You will encounter forks in the roads and opportunities—or, quests if you will—granted by others. Deciphering whether they feel aligned with your spirit is a lesson in discovering what nourishes your spirit. Over time, you learn more about what serves you and what doesn't. A boundary is set to protect our peace, but it's not meant to keep others or ourselves away entirely. It may seem easier to build a wall around yourself to avoid any hardships, but the truth is that we do not always have control. Knowing our inner truth allows us to live as close to our spirit as possible and can be a constant reassurance, and honoring what it desires and what it denies is part of honoring and building trust with ourselves.

Establishing a grounding practice leads to the next stage of stillness, or meditation. The word *meditation* is defined by the Cambridge Dictionary as "the act of giving your attention to only one thing, either as a religious activity or as a way of becoming calm and relaxed." When speaking of a meditation practice, I am referring to meditation within a witchcraft practice. To me, a meditation practice within your magical craft not only feeds the spirit by connecting the mind and body, but it is also a catalyst for achieving a trance-like mindset for ritual. The act of meditation itself is one that can be practiced by others, but it is the method that is specific to various cultures and religions. During the 1970s, meditation practices gained popularity in the Western spirituality movement and have since been adopted by the wellness industry in the United States. Unfortunately, this adoption has resulted in the colonization and popularization of these practices, with little regard for their sacred origins and the people of the religions from which they originated.

Should you have a desire to learn any of these meditative practices, I recommend seeking out teachers that are active members of these communities. This avoids further white-washing of sacred traditions. As a Witch, we must remember that a lesson we learn is how we can better protect and heal our community, and decolonization is part of that practice.

ACTIVITY

Return to Me, Energy

In this ritual, we will call back our energy that has been dispersed throughout the day, allowing us to feel restored and present. After grounding our energy, we will focus our intention to the center of our body. As you focus your attention here, allow your body to relax. Be mindful of the thoughts that come and allow them to go. After a few breaths, chant the following as a soft whisper, or say it in your mind:

**Return to me,
my energy.**

As you begin to chant this incantation, say it with conviction. Imagine the source within your core growing with the energy returning to your body. With the Witch's eye, this can be a swirling ball of light, lightning, a cloud—however you visualize this represented. Practice this until you feel a sense of fulfillment with your misplaced energy restored to you.

On the Besom,
the Witch Flies

Spirit-flight, or hedge-crossing, refers to the Witch's journey through the liminal space in spirit form. I must clarify that when referring to *flight*, we are not speaking of the actual capability of flying. The reference to flight is a metaphor for allowing your spirit to leave your physical body and travel throughout the Otherworld. In the folklore of Witches, we see the mention of spirit-flight being the Witch's way of traveling to their celebrations with the Devil, making pacts, and retrieving charms and spells during these sabbaths. With the aid of their besoms, or in some cases on the backs of bewitched neighbors, it is a journey that opens a door to so much more.

A Witch can seek consolation with spirits, obtain knowledge, nurture relationships, and even perform spells within these liminal spaces. The Otherworld is where spirits present themselves to the Witch, and where the Witch may introduce themselves. They become familiar with one another, to foster relationships. These journeys can provide deep insight into how to best work with these spirits. During my flights, I find that communication with my spirits is more prominent, and the spells performed are more impactful. It's in these spaces that I feel most connected with my spirits, and no one session is ever the same as another. I have met the spirits of the plants I have incorporated in my practice, as well as meeting an ancestral spirit during a powerful ritual. During this time, spirits may share potent knowledge and provide healing, and when returning to the physical realm the Witch carries that with them along their path.

Spirit-flight is a practice that takes patience for the Witch to become acquainted with. These sessions can be incredibly powerful when we set intentions prior. There are a few methods to approaching this spirit traveling. There are deep-guided meditation practices, trance-work, and even plants to aid you in the crossing. The most common method found in folklore is the application of poisonous plants to aid in achieving flight, referred to as *flying ointment*. The Northampton County witch, Phoebe Ward, crafted this ointment from the grease of corpses. Witches from Georgia would craft their flight ointment from the fat of graveyard snakes due to the belief that their magical powers were descendants of the serpent from the Garden of Eden. The ointment formula was provided to the Witch to be rubbed on their foreheads and wrists to prep for flight. The ingredients would vary depending on what was available to the Witch, but many Witches held knowledge of utilizing herbs from their local gardens. Nightshades were among the most popular used for their hallucinogenic properties. Mandrake root, *Mandragora officinarum*, in plant lore is richly associated with the Witch and occultism, with its mind-altering abilities rooted throughout history. Men and women would sell their souls to the Devil over this magical plant and its abilities to find them love and gold. The folklore of this plant continues, but here we see it was a key ingredient for the flying ointment recipe during the Middle Ages.

To confidently work with this medicinal and magical plant, I highly recommend extending research and hands-on experience when handling any poisonous plants for magical or medicinal usages. Mandrake is potent in its abilities, but it is also not commonly found here in North America. There are wonderful plant allies that are great replacements for mandrake, such as passionflower, mugwort, holy basil, skullcap, and lemon balm. A personal favorite blend that I have used for my flight sessions includes chamomile, lavender, lemon balm, and mugwort. I will prep this blend and sip mindfully for about an hour prior to my session to allow the herbs to work their magic. When it comes to any herbal crafting, understanding the herbs and their effects on our bodies and any medications is vital to practicing safely. Inquire with your doctor or another herbalist to see if these herbs will work for you. Everyone responds differently to herbs, and it is important to mention that if you are pregnant, nursing, on medication, or have any health concerns, it is especially important to refer to a physician's recommendations.

Aside from herbal crafting, there are charms that can provide support, like hag stones, or the witch-stone. Due to the stone's connection to water and being naturally eroded by its power, lore tells us that this charm can be used in spirit-flight as much as it can be used to protect against bewitchment reaching us during our sleep. The hag stone is the doorway to and from the Otherworld, with its naturally created hole through the stone. In Cornish tradition, the use of a hag stone was a common practice among Witches to connect with the Otherworld. To achieve this, the hag stone was fumigated with a special blend of incense and tied to a thread along with feathers. By swaying this thread over the smoke, the Witch would enter a trance-like state that facilitated a connection with the spirits. The incense served as an offering, which was exchanged for granted wishes made by the Witch.

We can find these stones on coastlines and gather them for spirit-flight charms and talismans. I will charm my hag stone with an incense blend of mugwort and lavender, speaking an incantation over it for protection granted by my spirits, and place it underneath my pillow as I prep for my flight session.

There are liminal spaces that are ideal for entering the Otherworld, as mentioned. In these spaces is where I feel magic is alive and well, available to all who wander through. The liminal space represents the in-between of our physical realm and the Otherworld—to feel, see, touch, and hear the whispers of spirits waiting for an introduction. Graveyards, caves, hedge rows, mountain tops, and fields of crops are all spaces that hold a sense of wonder and magic. Visiting these places can amplify the Witch's attempt to travel to the Otherworld. As you wander through your own fields and woods, do you feel it? Do you feel as if there is a shift? That perhaps if you allowed yourself to step in, you may wander into another realm?

A personal favorite experience that I shared with a dear friend of mine was in the Appalachian Mountains. We had just finished an ancestral ritual, and as we started to venture back to our vehicle by the short trail, we found ourselves in a part of the woods that was not familiar. The trail was easy for us to follow in, but as we followed it out it seemed to have shifted. Appalachian folk know that the woods encompass countless hauntings and unknown beings. I remember holding my breath; my body could sense that the world around me was not the one I was so familiar with. My friend looked up and asked for assistance, to which a raven in a nearby pine tree responded by cawing and flying in the opposite direction. We followed, and quickly found ourselves back to what looked familiar, the path that led us in appearing before us. It was frightening at first, but I found that those woods may have had something else in mind for us that evening.

History and lore show us time and time again that the Witch incorporates movement and chanting into their ritual to harness energy and travel between realms. A popular depiction of this ritual is from the famous collection of witch trials in *The History of Witches and Wizards* by W.P. written in 1720. This compendium of witch trials provides an image of the Witch dancing in a circle with their coven and the Devil, an illustration that captures the endless tales of the Witch's sabbaths. Walpurgis Night, a German celebration the night of April 30, is yet another tradition in which Witches gathered around a bonfire, dancing in celebration with one another. In German folklore, it was believed that on this night the Witches gathered to fly off into the hills to meet with the Devil after their dancing festivity. This lore was written in *The Malleus Maleficarum*, a collection of demonology literature from the fifteenth century that would later serve as a weapon during the European witch trials.

Let Us Fly

Spirit-flight allows us to enter a magical realm that is quite beneficial to the Witch. Here I will lay out a personal approach to spirit-flight that you can practice. Be patient with yourself, as some may have a more difficult time than others. With the help of visualization, meditation, and even music, we can explore the Otherworld in our spirit form.

Begin by creating a safe, dim-lit space, such as your personal bedroom, to help relax the mind. Laying down is a personal favorite position when hedge-crossing, but feel free to find a position that works for you. This is an important factor when it comes to flight, as any tension can be distracting. I suggest having a lit candle or dim night light nearby, as this will be helpful when returning to your physical body.

Once you have the space ready and are in a comfortable position, direct your attention to your breathing. Breathing methods come in handy when relaxing the mind and body. My personal favorite is inhaling for five counts and then out for five counts. Do this a few times until you regulate your breathing into a consistent rhythm.

Take root in your body at this time, focusing on the space between your physical body and the surface. Imagine your physical body taking roots here, knowing that it is safe where you are laying. You may find it helpful to recite, "I am safe," to ease any anxiety. Repeat this as often as needed.

Once you have your breathing nice and slow, focus your attention on your spirit form. You may feel a tingling sensation here. Visualize your spirit form lifting from your physical body, walking toward a tree in front of you. This can be any tree of your liking, but this will be the space that you continue to visit to explore the Otherworld. Another option would be to imagine a house. Decipher which visualization resonates with you more and which you prefer to visualize as your safe space to explore the Otherworld.

Practice visiting your tree or house in spirit form to become familiar with spirit-flight. Over time, you will learn the ways in which you can explore the Otherworld and become comfortable. A personal favorite time for this ritual is on the Full Moon, with it's strong energetic pull to explore the liminal.

The Art of Spellcrafting

Magic is already alive. It is the soil beneath your feet as you trek along in the neighboring woods. It is the fungi emerging from the moist ground, reaching to the trees above that extend beyond the hills and mountains, meeting the stars and sky. It is the first breath in the morning as the Sun peaks behind the blinds, and the relief of our daily caffeine intake. It lives within the ebbs and flows of our everyday life that many dismiss. For so long, magic was believed to be an evil source of power that only the feared could conjure and was used strictly to harm enemies and neighbors. But magic is beyond that. It can be healing and restoring to our spirit and to our communities. It can shine light on the good that would otherwise be hidden in the shadows. It can restore faith in ourselves when we are on the edge of our deepest depths. Magic can be the hand that reaches for ours when we are on the cliffs of no return. It is enduring, curious, and wildly freeing.

Magic was believed to only live in children's fairytale books. There was no magic that lived in any other world. It was strictly fantasy, and believing it otherwise was deemed odd and unrealistic. But the Witch sees the magic before their very own eyes. The way their spirit sings brings attention to the unfolding of events felt prior to their happening. It's the moment when we close our eyes and whisper, *I knew it*. It is the answered prayers sung to our ancestors, deities, and spirits. Magic is embedded in our spirit and invoked by our ways. It is inherently simple, yet a complexity beyond placing precise instructions on paper.

Magic is the intertwining of all things the Witch does, with intention threaded in. That is what makes it complex to define, as it all comes down to the individual Witch and their personal practice. Like a recipe, the casting of magic creates a ripple effect in our physical world. The ingredients and method may vary, but the goal remains the same—to achieve a desired wish.

There are some ceremonial approaches that the Witch may incorporate into their own practice. In Doreen Valiente's book *An ABC of Witchcraft, Past and Present*, she writes: "The magic circle is part of the general heritage of magical practice, which is worldwide and of incalculable age. Magic circles have varied from the elaborate spiritual fortress of divine names, which may be used by the ceremonial magician, to the simple round drawn the witch." The use of creating a circle around the Witch can be found in numerous magical practices. Within traditional witchcraft, there is the Compass Rite spoken about by Robert Cochrane. This ritual creates a sacred circle for invoking the spirits of the four corners and elements of nature along with our spirits and deities. The exact instruction of Cochrane's Compass Rite incorporates the tools belonging to the Witch, such as their stang and a cauldron, and mandates the ritual be performed outdoors. The layout looks like three circles from the center in which the Witch enters with their cauldron and stang. Each of the circles represents the level of Otherworld and creates a doorway entrance into accessing the other realms. Making your way inward to the center, starting from the north, which corresponded to the Witch Father, the first circle cast around would be of salt, the second of ash, and the last, water. Other ways of creating a sacred circle around the Witch may vary depending on the individualism of the practitioner and their traditions. However, we can conclude that the purpose remains the same—to create a safe space for the Witch to enter the Otherworld with their spirits and to aid in the magical working performed within the circle.

While some practitioners may incorporate more ceremonial practices, a folkloric traditional Witch may reference their own ancestral spirits' approaches. These ways may be simpler in tactic. In many folk practices, there was no time for casting circles for a spell. And in most cases, a spell was not regarded as a spell at all. Instead, it was a prayer from the Book of Psalms gifted by a great-grandmother over a cup of tea to cure a chest cold. This was viewed as more practical and simple and incorporated their religious beliefs. It was more about integrating magic into the mundane actions for practical solutions, then and now. When and how you decide to create a sacred space for spell crafting is entirely up to you and the intention set. In my personal practice, I establish a sacred space when I am calling on the help of another spirit. It becomes a door between the physical realm and the spiritual, allowing energies to flow through more easily.

Creating a Sacred Space

I will share with you my personal approach in creating a sacred space. The purpose is to establish that my spirit and body are safe in the place I will be performing a magical act and connecting to the energies of the Otherworld. It is a way to separate the magic from the mundane and establish energetic boundaries.

Begin by sitting in a quiet place. Focus on grounding your energy and quieting the mind, releasing any tension in your body, and achieving a level of comfort and relaxation.

Visualize here a hedge forming around you, encompassing you inside this circle formation. The hedge is tall and thick, separating you from the outside world. With this visualization, speak the following in your mind or outloud:

Within these walls, I create a safe space for my body and spirit. No spirit may enter unless I grant permission. In this space, I set the intention to _____. I am safe. I am present. Let these natural walls encompass me until I claim otherwise.

Now you have energetically created a safe space to perform your spells or for hedge-crossing. After you perform the magical act you intended, return to the center and visualize these walls coming down slowly. This ritual is one I use for more of a grand gesture, such as workings for large life shifts with the help of other spirits. Otherwise, much of my spell casting involves the folk ways in which establishing a sacred space is not needed.

The Witch's Altar

The Witch's altar is a space that directly reflects the practicing of the Witch. It is where they may commune with their spirits as well as craft their spells and other magical materials. In some cases, the Witch may acquire numerous altars, ranging from indoors to outdoors. It is tempting to put an altar in every room, each serving its own purpose. You may have an altar designated for your magical workings, while others, like an ancestor altar, are designated for other intentions or spirits. If you have a fireplace within your home, you may create an altar for your house on the mantle above the hearth. If you partake in kitchen witchery, designating an area within the kitchen for your magical tools can be yet another sacred space. This space should be a leveled, secure space that can allow you to place the items deemed necessary for the intention behind the altar for safety reasons. While some Witches may have a few altars within their home, nature offers another space. A garden altar or a designated tree stump can be used for outdoor workings and dedicated to the local spirits. Over the years, my personal altar has shifted to correspond with the shifts in my practice and the world around me. What first started as a small bedside table has grown into a family heirloom desk adopted from the marketplace that sits in the corner of my room with an apothecary shelf above, and shelves around, holding an array of witchcraft and folklore books. Following your intuition of where to establish your altar will undoubtedly be the best space for it.

Gathering the Witch's Tools

There are some tools that will be useful for the Witch's craft. Some can be acquired by purchase, while others can be crafted by hand or foraged from the land. It is up to you how you'd like to obtain these tools and what speaks to you. When gathering the tools, follow your inner knowing of what feels right. While some Witches will acquire the tools listed below, some may not resonate with some items and their usage. That is entirely valid. As you work with these tools, get to know their spirits and how they can be an aid in your spells. If you find that one tool feels better than the other, replace it with what works. The lovely thing about crafting your magical practice is that the tools will shift and change as you grow into defining what works well for you.

When foraging for tools, remember to consider your own ethics when acquiring from nature. Nature is already so giving, and the last thing a Witch does is take advantage. If in search for a tool, such as a stick or stang, speak the request to your local land and provide an opportunity for it to present the stick to you. It may not be the first one you stumble upon during your walk. You will know when it feels right. Your intuition will ring and your spirit will sing. These tools are a gift from spirits or deities. Express gratitude for gifting you this magical tool.

KNIFE: The blade of a knife can come in handy when we need to carve symbols and sigils into some material, like candles. The knife also represents the element of air. The sharpness of the blades can be used to energetically cut things away. My knife was purchased from a craftsman at my local Renaissance faire. I adored the simplicity of it, with its wooden handle and steel blade. I often find myself using it for measuring and cutting cords and carving into my candles with caution.

BESOM: One of my personal favorite tools, the besom, is a classic symbol of the Witch and is used for spirit-flight. I have two besoms at my altar—one is handmade and the other is a smaller store-bought version found during the autumnal season. The large besom is used as a hedge-crossing tool during ritual, while the other is used for cleansing purposes. After each shower, I sweep the besom across my body to energetically cleanse my spirit after a physical cleanse. It can also be used to sweep away stagnant energy at my altars during a routine cleanse, or for other purposes such as protection, when anointed with oil.

CAULDRON: Yet another symbolic tool commonly associated with the Witch, the cauldron represents the element of fire, a symbolism of creation and the hearth of the home. They come in all different materials and sizes. This tool may be best found purchased at your local store or from a local business. The material of your cauldron should be fire-safe, as it will hold hot coals and other ingredients that will burn your intentions to the Otherworld by smoke. Some Witches, such as myself, may have multiple cauldrons. I have one that I found at a local thrift shop made of copper. It is the one I use for my spells. The other is a cast-iron pot used within kitchen witchery and for brews. Cauldrons can also be used to burn loose incense for spells and rituals.

CUP: This might seem like a mundane tool to have at the altar, but as we discussed before, liquid offerings are an option when connecting with spirits. This cup can be designated for such offerings to the spirits you work with at your altar, whether that be your ancestors, deities, familiars, or others. Liquid offerings can be refreshed every few days or left to be evaporated and replaced with a new beverage. This tool can also be used as a divinational tool for scrying. Lastly, it can be something that you take along with you for outside rituals.

STAFF OR STANG: The staff or stang is a tool commonly used within traditional witchcraft practices. This tool is often a tall, forked branch and frequently resembled the Devil across folklore. It represents the element of earth and allows us to ground ourselves when performing rituals. It is a tool that can be used to direct energy during spells and in casting the Compass Rite. This is often acquired by foraging your local land. Visit somewhere that resonates with you, where you often spend time. Ask the spirits to guide you to the staff that is to be used in your magical practice. The type of wood will vary depending on your region, but some are known to be associated with the Witch like the oak, pine, hawthorn, and elder.

MORTAR AND PESTLE: This is a handy tool to have at your altar for workings that require combining magical herbs together to create a Witch's powder. This tool can be made up of different materials such as wood and marble. The one I have acquired is marble, and is set at my space ready to use when a powdered concoction needs to be grinded or simply mixed together, like an incense blend.

APOTHECARY: With jars labeled with their containments and stored nearby, an apothecary for the Witch is one that includes their magical herb allies. I include this because many Witches I personally know, including myself, have an inclination for herbal remedies and working with plants. Having an apothecary as a tool for my magical practice keeps me organized. It includes herbs that are used frequently, while having room for new allies to practice with. Your apothecary can include dried herbal ingredients in jars, herbal oils and concoctions. It is a space of healing and aid. See page 89 for the Witch's Apothecary Cabinet.

CANDLES: When I think of the ancestors before me who practiced witchery, I recall the conditions in which they worked. Candles were used as a light source and found in sacred spaces like churches. Whether you have tapered candles, tealights, or even LED candles, it sets the tone around this magical working space. To write, cast a spell, or perform a ritual by candlelight creates a peaceful atmosphere for the spirit. Candles can also be used in many spells and during rituals to work with the energy of fire.

THE WITCH'S GRIMOIRE: A grimoire encompasses your rituals, spells, charms, incantations, rites, and anything you will use in your magical practice. My grimoire is a simple notebook with scribbles of entries written after spirit-flight, formulas for spells, incantations, and many other formulas for my craft. Choose a book that feels right to you. This can be a journal, a notebook, a sketchbook—any type of book that you will cherish. It does not need to be perfect to begin composing your grimoire. Keep note of what worked with each spell, charm, rite, or other ritual manifested for future reference.

OTHER TRINKETS: As you build your altar space, you may come across other tools that will play a role in your practice. These tools can be bones, stones, or other foraged material. It is entirely up to the Witch what they find useful in their magical workings. Bones can be sourced ethically from an animal that represents your familiar or one that you feel a spiritual connection with. Stones can be used to represent a special place you once visited that you'd like to return to or connect to during a ritual. Other imagery will vary depending on what is prominent in your magical practice, a representation of something symbolic that is important to you.

Putting the "Craft" in Witchcraft

As we gazed around the Witch's lair earlier, we came across bottles filled with unknown containments, knotted yarn hung near doorways, and candles dressed in Witch's powder. There is something to be said about the "craft" part of witchcraft. It is where inspiration lives. The mind of the Witch can find creativity in observing the materials they have on hand. Witchcraft wasn't as mainstream in the past as it is in the modern days of the New World. When it was looked down upon and accused of evil, witchcraft was often done discreetly. Only in the quiet chambers of the Witch's home could one find any evidence of witchery, and even then, skeptics would question. Look around at where you are sitting at this moment. I am sure that you can pick up something in arms reach to be used in a spell. Think beyond the containments of how we think it *should* look and follow instead how it *feels*. There are mundane items that I use every day that are perfect for a spell. You just have to get a little creative.

THE WITCH'S BOTTLE: The first Witch's bottle discovered in England was in the seventeenth century. The material of the bottle was either glass or stone. The containments varied from items such as iron nails, hair, fingernail clippings, and perhaps even urine. It was believed this spell was used as a decoy for bewitchment—whatever spell casted unto the individual would be captured and destroyed by the Witch's bottle. The bottle would be hidden underneath floorboards and within the chimney walls of the home. Today, a modernized version of the Witch's bottle can contain herbal allies, vinegar, nails, and any personal talisman of the Witch to be used as a decoy. It can be stored at the altar or in a discreet space within the home.

NEEDLE AND THREAD: Needlecrafting is an art where needle meets fabric, a form of knot magic. This craft is intentional, from laying out the plan to choosing the fabric and weaving the threads. Needlecrafting includes quilting, knitting, crocheting, embroidery, and any other craft that utilizes sewing. With each stitch, an intention is made. The Witch can weave their magic into a fabric piece for a specific desire, entering a trance-like mindset with the repetitive handwork.

POPPETS/SPELL DOLLS: A poppet, or spell doll, is found across Europe to be used in sympathetic magic. Whatever is done to the poppet is manifested in the physical world of the individual it represents. Poppets can be crafted with moldable material like clay or dough, or crafted by fabric and needle. It can be done simply by just forming it into the shape of a person or intricately replicating the individual from physical features to clothing (perhaps even containing elements such as the person's hair).

CANDLES: Whether hand-dipped or store-bought, candles are one of the most popular forms of fire magic. Beyond being used simply as a tool for light, they can be dressed with a Witch's powder or with other herbal allies for a specific intention. Each color of a candle represents a specific intention—white for purification, black for banishment, yellow for joy, orange for creativity, red for passion, pink for love, purple for divination, and blue for healing. Names, sigils, and other symbols can be engraved in the candle to enchant it with a specific intention or for someone specific.

CHARM BAGS: Made of cloth or other fabric material, these enchanted bags were used by the cunning-folk and healers to cure illnesses for their friends, family, and fellow neighbors. Within the bag, containments included written charms and herbal allies for a specific intention. The charm bag was to be worn or carried with the individual for a set number of days instructed.

WITCH'S OIL: These anointments can be created to be consumed or not, but caution is to be had when using for consumption. The containment of an oil or tincture typically includes an array of herbal allies for their magical properties. Some of them contain just one herbal ally, while others can be a blend, each with their own medicinal and magical usages. When crafting a tincture, a spirit or liquor will used with the intention of medicinal use. When crafting an an oil, a carrier oil is chosen, such as olive oil, coconut, grape seed, and others. The decision may be based on shelf-life and purpose. The oil can be used to anoint the self and magical tools.

WITCH POWDER: This powder is to be used during rituals and other spells to raise energy and establish a spiritually safe space. Ingredients vary depending on the magical correspondences of each herbal ally. Ingredients are gathered into a mortar and pestle to be ground into a fine powder. The powder can be cast into the fire during spells, sprinkled within the Witch's space to establish an energy boundary, or sprinkled and then swept away to remove negative energies.

POTIONCRAFTING: Beverages that are brewed can be enchanted with magic from the Witch. With ingredients corresponding to specific intentions, the Witch can create infused syrups, tea blends, and more, with their herbal knowledge. Each step of potioncrafting is an opportunity for enchantment, from the tea blend, brew, or beverage of choice to the making and the consumption. You can stir in your intentions with a spoon and speak an incantation over the potion.

SIGILS AND SYMBOLS: Sigil crafting is a unique way of encompassing an intention or petition into a symbol that your spirit will recall intuitively when visualizing it. There are many ways to go about sigil crafting. Each Witch will have their preference. The goal remains the same in that a petition is written out. From this phrase, symbols are created to represent the stated petition. For example, "I am protected" can be written out for the Witch to draw a symbol inspired by this petition. The sigil is then used to be carved into candles, drawn on windows with blessed water, and other ways to use the sigil's magical energy.

INCANTATION WRITING AND SPOKEN CHARMS: Words have power. When spoken with conviction, the energy behind every spoken word cannot be ignored. Spoken charms can be found in magic across Europe. In some folk practices, spoken charms can include verses from the Bible. There are others found within the origins of your ancestral spirits and in their ancestral language. They are a prayer to the cosmic. Incantation writing is a personal practice. Some incantation writing can be done during ritual, allowing intuitive writing to play a part in this trance-like state.

THE WITCH'S APOTHECARY CABINET

The Witch will often find themselves incorporating herbal knowledge into their craft. It happens naturally as we connect with the plant allies in our surrounding place. Each plant ally has a magical use as well as their own medicinal purposes. Nature has a funny way of offering medicinal solutions throughout the seasonal shifts. Here in North America, much of our knowledge today comes from Indigenous Peoples that have resided here long before us. We can keep this wisdom safe by practicing ethical foraging and herbal remedies, by not overharvesting medicinal plants, protecting endangered species, and paying respect to the native plants that remain sacred to Indigenous Peoples.

In addition, the herbal allies we use in spells can be found within our own kitchen cabinets. They do not necessarily have to be foraged by hand. Listed below are some personal plant allies that I find myself utilizing in my magical workings. Some of these herbal friends have been used for both magical and medicinal usages, but because I am a self-taught herbalist, I recommend the Witch seeks a physician or clinical herbalist with much more knowledge in how they might use the following medicinally. The following correspondence list is compiled from my personal experiences with each ally. If you find a particular spell calls for an ingredient that you do not have present, feel free to replace it with any of the following correspondents. I encourage the Witch to personally experiment with each herb for themselves.

CALENDULA: healing, fresh start, cleansing

CHAMOMILE: soothe anxiety within mind and body, aid in money matters

CINNAMON: dispel bewitchment, protection of money matters

COFFEE: inspiration in creativity, speed up results, increase finances

CORNFLOWER: aid in divination, increase intuition

BASIL: clear confusion, luck in wealth and opportunities, ward against evil spirits

BAY: wish fulfillment, increase energy

GARDEN SAGE: purifying and cleansing

GARLIC: ward off negativity and unwanted spirits, strengthen body and spirit

HAWTHORNE: healing matters of the heart, protection, spiritual connection

JUNIPER: truth reveal of self and protection against mischief

LAVENDER: aid in sleep and dreamwork, soothing for matters of the mind

LEMON BALM: aid in courage, speaking what's on your mind and heart

MUGWORT: spirit-flight and connecting to the Otherworld

NETTLE: protection against negative energy, connect to ancestral spirits

PASSIONFLOWER: aid in connection (platonic or romantic)

ROSEMARY: mental clarity, ward against negativity, cleansing out the old

ROSE (DRIED, CULINARY): self-love and self-empowerment

ROSEHIPS: attraction, healing

THYME: purifying, protection of the house and health

YARROW: healing matters of protection against ill-will

VALERIAN: clear miscommunication, welcome harmony into space and situations

VERVAIN: banish away negative energy, cleansing, spiritual connection

THE WITCH'S CALENDAR

The Witch is attuned to the natural world, embracing the freshness of Spring, the vitality of Summer, the nostalgia of Autumn, and the quietness of Winter. They recognize that nothing is permanent and that the wheel keeps turning. This serves as a gentle reminder that, like nature, we are constantly shedding layers as time passes. With each passing season comes an opportunity to learn a valuable lesson, as if a knock on our door saying, "It's that time again." The natural rhythm of each cycle holds energy that we can tap into. Witchcraft is deeply connected to the earth and the seasons, allowing us to intuitively understand and connect with their shifts. These cycles often mirror our inner world, and as we deepen our connection to our surroundings, we begin to resonate with the changes in the air.

When it comes to creating the Witch's Calendar for the traditional witch, I welcome the conversation of developing your own by looking to your local folklore and connecting to the place. There are undeniably days throughout the year that resonate with the Witch, such as All Hallows' Eve, but there is something to say when we listen to our land in how we can best honor the cycles around us. Perhaps you live somewhere that doesn't experience all the seasons. To dismiss what nature is sharing with us for the sake of following a set date in seasonal shifts is disregarding the wisdom that is being shown—a missed opportunity for spiritual connection with the land that is vital for the Witch. With climate change obvious to our eyes now, we can see that the dates on the calendar may not entirely reflect what is happening outside our window. The solstices and equinoxes are calculated by the Sun, but the leaves on the trees may be earlier or later depending on location.

Researching the local folklore of our place can lead to a discovery of unique celebrations specific to our home. In my hometown, there is an annual apple festival at the beginning of every September. A time of honoring the fruits of our labor. It was not written in books of witchcraft or spiritualism. Instead, it was the curiosity and connection I had to where I rooted much of my practice. This honorary celebration came from the ancestries of my local community. There is nothing more rewarding than connecting with your local community and integrating seasonal celebration into the making of the Witch's Calendar. However your calendar looks, the purpose is the same powerful time for the Witch to connect with the Otherworld, commune with spirits, and connect with the magic of the natural world around them.

Seasonal Cycles

SPRING EQUINOX: new beginnings, the start of something, fertility of projects/ideas/self, awakening, increase, renewal, healing

SUMMER SOLSTICE: growth, abundance, nurture, strength, partnership, celebration

AUTUMNAL EQUINOX: reflection, celebrating fruits of labor, hearth, transformation, gratitude, honoring the dead

WINTER SOLSTICE: banish, self-work, Otherworld, intuition, endings, grounding, solitude, exploring emotional depths, life cycle

FOR THE GRIMOIRE

The Witch's Calendar

Visit your local library or even the website of your town. Research annual and seasonal celebrations and festivals. Take note of any that resonate with you. Do you have lavender farms nearby? Do they host any celebrations throughout the year? Perhaps you have apple farms like I did in my own hometown. The agriculture of our place can have an influence on the local festivities that occur.

Create a wheel to craft your own calendar. If integrating traditional harvest festivals from your ancestral origins, feel free to include them here. Make note of their origins, the customs that the people have, and how you may celebrate them today.

The Witch's Clock

There's no denying that the Witch has an intimate connection with a friend in the sky—the Moon. We see it throughout historical documentations of the Witch and their relationship with rituals under the moonlit sky. Corresponding our magic with the cycles in season and with the Moon allows us to call upon their virtues. At each turn of the wheel, we flow with the tide of nature's waves. Each season and lunar cycle introduces a new wave of energy to aid us in our magical workings. It is magical beyond explanation when we harness the Moon's influence.

FULL MOON: The energy of the Full Moon is potent. It is most known for being the ideal time for the Witch to cast a spell or perform a rite or ritual. The moonlight shines down just enough to make shapes and forms among the trees, highlighting the path for the Witch. It is mesmerizing, and so many Witches resonate with the Full Moon. As one side is illuminated, there remains the opposite side hidden in the dark—unknown, unseen. This time is particularly effective for most intentions.

accomplishment, activation, intuition, divination, empowerment, illumination, power, transformation, strength

WANING MOON: From the Full Moon, the shadow begins to shift as it dips into the Dark Moon. Some may experience this time to be more tiring, or as a time to recover from the energetic Full Moon.

banishment, bind, protection, purification, release, reversals, retreat/rest, resolutions to underlining problems

NEW MOON: The Dark Moon calls for internal journeying. The night is dark with no moonlight; a symbolic time for exploring the darkness. It is an opportunity for connecting to our own depths. It can also be a time for spirit-flight into the Otherworld, connecting with our spirits, familiars, and ancestors. The New Moon is a chance to reconnect with ourselves.

Otherworld, renewal/rebirth, self-awareness, emotional connection to self, spirit work, beginnings

WAXING MOON: From the Dark Moon, we begin to see the luminous light on the Moon once again as it regains its power. Some may experience this time to be more driven and energy boosting.

creativity, growth, increased energy, motivation, passion

PART 2
THE WITCH'S ESSENTIAL SPELLS

CHAPTER 4

FOR THE WITCH'S SPIRIT

The spirit of the Witch, as we have discussed, is such a vital relationship for a spiritual path. It is the essence of who we are. It is how we connect in a deep, profound way with other spirits. It guides us through our every day and even within the Otherworld. Because of this, it is important to nourish and nurture it. By doing this, we can ensure that we are cleansed and protected against any unwanted or unwell energies from outside sources. It is also an opportunity to strengthen our spiritual connection with ourselves. In this chapter, I will present a series of spells and rituals to be used with your spirit in mind. Throughout my personal journey, I have used these exact spells and rituals to aid me in healing, nourishing, protecting, and creating intentions for the life I desire. Let them inspire you and your own craft.

Cord-Cutting Candle

The Lore

In the Middle Ages, Europeans crafted their candles by dipping them into melted animal fat before beeswax was introduced. The candle-making process was soon replaced by beeswax, as it was a much cleaner burn versus the smokey flame the animal fat would produce. Candles were the main source of light during this time and were often found within people's homes as well as in sacred rituals.

The Spell

This cord-cutting candle spell aids us in breaking free from old patterns. Throughout my personal healing journey, I felt inspired to "break free" from certain behaviors, thoughts, and people. You may do this during the Full Moon or Waning Moon.

There are a few options to go about this spell. Here we will discuss one option with store bought candles.

1 white candle to represent yourself

1 black candle to represent what/ who you are breaking free from

A strand of your hair, optional

Carving tool or sewing needle

A pair of scissors

Fire-proof plate or cast-iron skillet, somewhere safe to contain the candles

A lighter

8-inch / 20-cm cord

For the candle that will represent you, take the candle and knock it awake on the counter or rub it in between your hands. You may take a hair strand of yours to tie around this candle, but this is optional. You may carve your name into the candle otherwise. Take the other candle and knock it awake or rub it in between your hands. With your carving tools or sewing needle, carve into it what you are wanting to disconnect from. This can be a word like "self-sabotage," or it could be a phrase about a negative belief you want to disconnect from.

Within a fire-proof plate or a cast-iron skillet, light the bottom of one of the candles to melt it just a bit and place it on the surface, then light the bottom of the other and place it beside the other candle, about two inches (5 cm) apart.

Or, place them in candle handles about four inches (10 cm) apart.

Take the eight-inch (20-cm) cord and wrap the two candles together. Tie the cord so that it is secure in place. Then, charge your spell by rubbing your hands together and projecting energy while stating the incantation:

The cord between you and me,
will catch fire and set me free.

Light the two candles and allow them to burn all the way down in a safe environment. With the scissors in hand, visualize the energy between the two candles. Then, with conviction, cut the cord, severing the energetic tie between the two. Allow the candles to burn all the way down.

If you'd like to craft your own candles, you may follow the instructions below. Though handcrafting our tools is not necessary for an impactful spell, it does allow an opportunity to be more mindful of infusing the crafted tools with our attention and energy.

100% beeswax or beeswax pellets

Candle pour container, found at your local craft store

Wax paper

Taper candle mold

Cotton candle wick

Cooking spray

Cooking thermometer

Scissors

Begin by melting your beeswax slowly within the candle pouring container on the stovetop on medium heat. Be careful not to let it boil, as you do not want to let it get too hot. While the beeswax is melting, prep the area by placing a few sheets of wax paper nearby. Thread the taper candle mold with the cotton candle wick, leaving room at the top to pull the candle out from the mold. Spray the mold with cooking spray to make retrieving the candle easier.

Remove the melted beeswax from the stove and allow to cool until about 140° F (60° C). Then, pour slowly into the taper candle mold. Allow it to cool completely, about one hour. Remove the candle from the mold and store in a cool, dry place.

Spell Maintenance

To dispose the remnants of this spell, simply throw away the wax remains into the trash. Wax is not environmentally friendly, so disposing it properly is important. Clean the surface as necessary.

See image on page 94.

LOVE THYSELF POTION

THE LORE

The rose represents the beauty of duality with tales between lovers and death.
It is a plant that is closely tied to witch-lore across many cultures, including
stories of the rose assisting spirits crossing over the veil and being a comfort to
those they left behind in the physical world. The symbolism of a rose was used
in important buildings such as council chambers across Europe as a reminder
that what was spoken was to remain private. In lore, you will find that the rose
represents lovers, a plant that intertwines two together. From these stories, we
understand the rose as a versatile plant ally, used for protection against heart-
aches, to tie us to our significant others, and as a connection to other spirits.

THE SPELL

To begin, spend some time connecting with the rose. Focus on the plant's
energy and how it feels to you (see page 30). Once you feel familiar with the
rose's energy, we will gather the remaining ingredients that will be used for
this potion.

1–2 tbsp / 5–11 g of all-natural,
unsweetened cocoa powder

2 cups / 480 ml of milk or dairy-
free milk

1 tsp / 5 ml of honey

½ tbsp / 4 g of cinnamon

A pinch of cayenne pepper, optional

Dried culinary-grade rose petals, to
garnish

Begin crafting your potion by combining the all-natural unsweetened cocoa
powder and milk or dairy-free milk. Set on medium low heat and stir consistently. Once combined, add the honey to sweeten. Then add the cinnamon. If
interested in adding some additional protection energy and some heat, add the
cayenne pepper. Combine altogether for about 2 to 3 minutes, until warmed
and well stirred. Pour the potion into a mug.

With the dried roses, say the following incantation as you sprinkle some on top as a garnish:

Oh Rose, I ask of you—

Open my heart,
To my love from the start.
Heal the wounds inflicted upon me,

From those I know and those I do not see.

As you sip this potion, spend some time somewhere that you enjoy, whether that is in the comfort of your bedroom, living space, altar, or even somewhere outside like your garden. Prepare this potion beforehand and take it with you. Sip mindfully, visualizing a light around you as you consume. Speak kindly to yourself as you consume.

Speaking Kindly to Yourself

Here are some things to consider speaking out loud or in your mind as you sip your potion:

I am brave for overcoming difficult seasons in my life.
I am worthy of good things.
I am a beautiful being and my light shines bright.
My heart is kind and others see that.

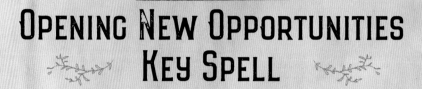

Opening New Opportunities Key Spell

The Lore

In Appalachian lore, the horseshoe was a tool to repel the Devil. In colonial times, folks would place a horseshoe above the door of their barn to protect their cattle against witchery. The iron material drove away any bewitchment and was a strong material for protection. Where I am from in these mountains, placing the horseshoe facing up meant that the good luck of the family was contained. If the horseshoe were to tip over and face down, all the good luck would pour out.

The Spell

Consider casting this spell on the New Moon, the marking of new beginnings. When you are in need of opening up new opportunities, this spell will assist in opening the doors.

A horseshoe

Paper

Pen or pencil

Road opening oil; this can be purchased at a local metaphysical store

Cord or green thread

1 bay leaf

Begin by cleansing the horseshoe. With your paper and pen or pencil, write the incantation three times across the paper:

Open the door, to a world of more,
opportunities come forth to me, abundance, and prosperity.

Turn the paper slightly clockwise then write your full name three times across the incantation, signing the petition for new opportunities. Place three drops of road opening oil onto the petition, using your finger to rub the oil in a clockwise motion to charge the petition.

Then turn the paper clockwise again to fold towards you. As you fold, turn the paper clockwise after each fold for a total of three times.

With the cord, wrap the petition and bay leaf together around the center of the horseshoe with it facing up until it is secure, then tie a knot to finish the spell.

Place the horseshoe on your altar or somewhere safe where it will always face up. Every New Moon, you can recharge the spell by projecting new energy into it. Hold the horseshoe in your hands during a meditation session. Focus your attention on the horseshoe. With visualization, imagine you are standing in front of a door that slowly begins to open as you speak this incantation in your mind or out loud:

Open the door, to a world of more,
opportunities come forth to me,
abundance and prosperity.

Spell Maintenance

To dispose of the spell once the opportunity or opportunities have manifested, untie the knot that holds the petition to the horseshoe. Dispose of the cord into the trash. Take your petition and bay leaf to burn it in your cauldron, fireplace, a bonfire, or another safe place. As it burns and the smoke rises, give thanks to the spirits. Cleanse the horseshoe with either your besom, smoke, or with your own energy, and save it for another spell working or to place above your door, face-up, to bring good fortune into your home.

Rest Well Sleep Potion

The Lore

Chamomile is most commonly associated with its aid in prosperity workings. Gamblers would wash their hands with this herb before their games to increase their chances in luck. It has also been used to aid in protection and banishing against bewitchment or negativity entities by sprinkling the flowers around the property. Medicinally, chamomile is a great herb for aiding in sleep. Chamomile in baths is used to calm colic in babies. With its medicinal properties in aiding sleep, it can also help us magically with dreamwork. By sipping chamomile tea, the magical herbs relax our mind and body.

The Spell

This potion is best enjoyed in the evening prior to sleep to help relax the mind and body for a restful night.

1 tbsp / 2 g of dried chamomile flowers

1 tbsp / 5 g of lemon balm

½ tbsp / 2 g of passionflowers

½ tbsp / 2 g of dried culinary-grade rose petals

½ tbsp / 3 g spearmint

Bowl

Tea pot or tea strainer

Hot water

Honey, optional

Gather your dried herbs and bowl. For each ingredient, state its role in this tea blend as you place it into a bowl to combine:

Chamomile, bring forth to me a night of rest.
Lemon balm, bring forth to me a night of calm.
Passionflower, bring forth to me a night of ease.
Rose, bring forth to me a night free of heartache.
Spearmint, bring forth to me a night of slumber.

Once the tea blend is combined, place your hands over the blend and state the incantation:

With the aid of these herbs in this spell,
my body and mind will rest well.

Place this tea blend into a tea pot or strainer filled with hot water and steep for 3 to 5 minutes. When ready, sweeten with honey if you like.

Spell Maintenance

As with any herbal concoction, inquire with your physician and be aware of any allergies, as everyone responds to herbs differently. Use organic material to ensure herbs are safe for consumption.

THE WITCH'S PERSONAL POPPET

THE LORE

Poppets are used across many different cultures and crafted in different ways based on available materials. Poppets were used for sympathetic magic—to represent someone or something—and were often used by the Witch for healing or baneful magic. In England, they would craft the poppet out of cloth material, enchanting it with a talisman from their target like hair or nail clippings. Whatever was done to this poppet would manifest in the physical realm to the individual.

THE SPELL

Poppets can be used to create change for yourself as well as others. In this spell, we are crafting a poppet and various poppet beds for different intentions.

1 cup / 292 g of salt

2 cups / 250 g of flour

1 cup / 240 ml of water

Gingerbread person cookie cutter

Combine the salt and flour together in a mixing bowl. Then, add the water. Mix well until it becomes dough-like. Roll the dough out onto a floured surface to prevent it from sticking. Using the cookie cutter, cut out the shape of a person. Place the dough unto a foil-covered pan and bake at 250°F (120°C) for about 30 minutes, flipping it over once, about 15 minutes in. Allow to cool.

To wake up your poppet, say the following incantation with the poppet in your hands:

*Open your eyes, you will see
that you will now represent me.*

The poppet is now enchanted to represent you in this physical realm. Place the poppet somewhere safe, such as your altar or another safe space. When you are in need of something to manifest in your physical life, you can utilize the poppet to help.

Prosperity Poppet Bed

To attract prosperity into your physical realm, create this poppet bed on which to place your poppet.

A bowl big enough for the poppet to lay in

Uncooked rice (enough to fill up half the bowl)

A pinch of mint

3 cinnamon sticks

3 coins of your choice

Spiritually cleanse the bowl. Place the uncooked rice into the bowl, using enough to fill it about half way. Place the pinch of mint, 3 cinnamon sticks, and the 3 coins of your choice into the bowl. Place your poppet on top of the bowl. Rub your hands together, then place them over the bowl with your poppet, and state the incantation:

Manifest for me,
opportunities of prosperity.

Leave the poppet here to attract prosperous opportunities.

(continued)

Attraction Poppet Bed

To charm and attract others, create this poppet bed to place your poppet.

A bowl big enough to lay your poppet in

A handful of dried rose petals

A pinch of jasmine

A pinch of passionflower

Spiritually cleanse the bowl. Place the dried rose petals into the bowl, along with the jasmine and passionflower. Place your poppet in the bowl. With your hands over the bowl and poppet, state the incantation:

Direct their attention to me,
my charm and kindness, they will see.

Leave the poppet here for when you want to attract others' attention or charm others in a specific situation, like an interview, date, or otherwise.

Travel Protection Poppet Bed

Use this poppet bed to protect yourself during short or long-distance travels.

A bowl big enough for your poppet to lay in

A handful of salt

A pinch of cayenne pepper

A pinch of black peppercorns

A pinch of thistle

Spiritually cleanse the bowl. Place the salt to cover most of the bottom of the bowl, followed by a pinch of cayenne pepper, black peppercorns, and thistle. Lay your poppet on top. Place your hands over the bowl, and state the incantation:

Protect my peace and will,
from all events of ill.

Leave the poppet here in a safe space during the duration of your trip.

Spell Maintenance

You may recharge your poppet beds or poppet by reinstating the incantations. To safely dispose of your poppet, release the intention by stating:

I release you from your duties. The purpose has been fulfilled.

Dispose of the poppet by crumbling it using your mortar and pestle. Grind until it is a fine powder and use to empower future spells.

Let Me See Divination Oil

The Lore

Every Witch has their own unique ritual for divination as well as favored form of divination. For some, they practice in attire separate from their mundane clothing. They wash their hands and cover their head with a veil to protect themselves during communication. Divination practices vary between Witches, depending on the region their practice is inspired from.

The Spell

For this spell, we are crafting an oil to be used for divination. Craft this anointment oil under the Full Moon. This oil can be used as a tether between the Witch and the chosen divination method.

An empty glass bottle with a dropper, any size

A spoonful of cornflower

A spoonful of mugwort

Carrier oil of your choice

Combine the cornflower and mugwort into your glass bottle, then fill the bottle with your chosen carrier oil. Shake the ingredients awake by saying the following:

With this oil, I may clearly see
what the spirits share with me.

Use this oil prior to divination or spirit-flight to help open yourself up to interpreting the message from the Otherworld.

Spell Maintenance

Hands may be oily after use, so you may want to wash your hands afterwards. Be sure to use ingredients friendly for your skin if applying on hands.

See image on page 14.

Strengthen Friendship and Connection Potion

The Lore

The crab apple tree holds many stories of its connection to the Otherworld and spirits. The apple orchard countryside of England held the tradition of *wassailing*, which entailed singing to the oldest and wisest apple trees to ward off evil spirits, offering mulled cider and cakes at the base of their trunks in exchange for a fruitful year and good health. This cider was mixed with spices. The wassail queen would dunk their toast into the beverage and place it on the branches of the apple trees for the robins to enjoy, attracting good spirits.

The apple trees are wise spirits, and they can also aid in protection, love, and good health. If you cut an apple in half, you will see the Witch's pentagram formed by the seeds. The apple was used for protection spells while its seeds were used for divination methods. By sharing half an apple with someone else, it strengthens the connection between you and the other.

The Spell

With the apple being a fruit connecting to the Otherworld and between two people, this potion is crafted to share among individuals or spirits with whom you wish to strengthen your connection. Brew this in your cauldron, or stovetop pot, as an offering to the spirits or to share with loved ones.

6 cups / 1420 ml of organic apple cider

3 cinnamon sticks

1 tbsp / 8 g of ground cloves

1 tsp / 4 g of ground nutmeg

1 orange

Pour the organic apple cider, or enough to share among the people or spirits you wish to share it with, into a stovetop pot. Add the cinnamon sticks, ground cloves, and nutmeg. Peel and cut the orange into slices, then place it into the brew. Allow it to simmer on low to medium heat for about 5 to 7 minutes. Serve warm.

As you share it with your spirits or with other people, celebrate your connection by toasting:

> *To the kin between you and me,*
> *celebrate the love between.*
> *Thou rely on the other's shoulder,*
> *to pour out any bitter bother.*
> *Back-to-back, protected by each one*
> *In this chapter and the future to come.*

Drink the spiced cider with friends and/or kindred spirits.

THE WITCH'S LADDER FOR THE NEW YEAR

THE LORE

The Witch's Ladder was a tool believed to have belonged to a local Witch discovered in Somerset, England, and stored within the Pitt Rivers Museum. The Witch's Ladder hung in the attic of a woman's home, crafted together by rope and chicken feathers used for getting away with the neighbor's cow milk. Gemma Gary speaks about the Witch crafting together a thread with tied crow's feathers and a hag stone on the end to use for spirit work within Cornish folk traditions. By burning incense and fumigating the Witch's Ladder, the prayers spoken would reach the spirits. The Witch's Ladder was used for protection and spirit communication. Today, we can use this traditional charm for a variety of intentions with knot magic.

THE SPELL

Like the lore of the Witch's Ladder, items are knotted into the rope for a specific intention, whether that's to cast your prayers to the spirits or to grant desires or for protection. For this spell, the intention is to craft a Witch's Ladder for the upcoming new year. This can be made on the calendar New Year, your solar return (birthday), or on All Hallows' Eve, as the Witch often marks these days as the beginning of a new year. Decide when feels right to set new intentions for the upcoming year.

Consider what you would like to bring forth into the new year. For example, if you are wanting to unlock new opportunities, you may decide to use a key to represent this. If you want to bring forth joy and happiness, a dried orange is a good choice. If you want protection, consider a bone or a crow's feather. A hag stone would also be great for protection or to connect with the Otherworld. Contemplate on a few things that you wish to bring in along with some correspondences.

10-inch / 25-cm piece of cord, thread, or yarn

Items to represent your specific intention

Incense stick or loose incense

At one end of the cord or rope, tie a loop so that you can hang it near your altar space or within another safe space in your home.

Gather your items that represent each intention you would like to manifest within the next year. Choose which item to start with and tie it into the cord or rope. Then, work your way down the ladder, tying each item into it. Once you get to the bottom of the ladder, tie a knot three times.

Light your incense stick or loose incense. Fumigate the Witch's Ladder by swaying it over the smoke, allowing your prayers to be sent off into the Otherworlds as you speak the incantation:

> *The first knot begins the spell,*
> *of the desires I wish to tell,*
> *Let the (insert item) bring (intention),*
> *Let the (insert item) bring (intention) . . .*
> *(continue this list of items for your Witch's Ladder),*
> *The last knot ties it together,*
> *what will be will last forever.*

Spell Maintenance

As the following year unfolds and these desires manifest in the physical realm, unknot the specific intention that was granted. This releases the energy. If there is a desire that has not come to fruition after the first year, rework the Witch's Ladder and dispose of the old. Revisiting our desires allows us to reflect and recognize that we may not resonate with the previous stated desires any longer.

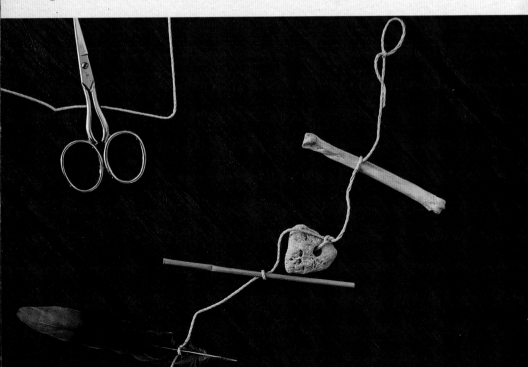

CHAPTER 5
FOR CLEANSING

One of the important factors in maintaining a spiritual hygiene routine is cleansing. Though it may seem simple, it is the most effective way for us to maintain a clean and safe spiritual space around us throughout our personal practice. When communing with other spirits or coming into contact with other practitioners, we may stumble upon an energy that lingers far longer than we desire. To counteract this, we can create a spiritual cleansing routine to clear away this energy that may disrupt our personal peace and interfere with our spiritual well-being. Do not let these simple spells fool you—the tools and items used hold so much potential magic and energy for cleansing away what does not serve us. Let them be a guide into crafting a cleansing routine that feels right to your own craft.

Begin the Day Spell

The Lore

Healing waters are found across many traditions in Great Britain. In Cornwall, wells were holy and a place for kindred spirits, a portal for the Otherworld. Healing spells for individuals and children were often performed at local holy wells. Individuals would either bathe in them or pass their children through the healing water. These wells, being linked to the Otherworld, were also a space to perform divination. The Witch would locate their local healing well to commune with spirits, opening themselves to the wisdom and knowledge the spirits shared.

The Spell

The spirit of water is cleansing and healing. The spirit of the local streams, creeks, and rivers may hold the same energy. As we develop a relationship with our local waters, we may be invited to take a dip, becoming part of their magical essence. For this spell, if you do not have access to a local stream or body of water but wish to establish this type of connection, we can use the water within our homes for this spell to cleanse away the old for a new day.

Half a handful of fresh or dried calendula

A bowl of water

A sprig of fresh rosemary

Put the calendula and rosemary into the bowl of water. Place your hands over the bowl of water and state the incantation:

Today, I start anew
washing away the old to help get me through
What the day ahead brings to me
With fresh eyes, I can see.

With one hand, stir the containments within the water clockwise. Visualize the herbs and water waking up. Connect and follow their energy. With both hands now, place them into the water to gather a handful. Wash your face with this water, head over the bowl.

Spell Maintenance

Once complete, return the water back to the Earth by disposing it outdoors away from your property to prevent old energies from lingering. Or, simply pour it down the drain, disposing the herbs separately into the trash as to not clog the sink. Give thanks to the spirits of the herbs and water. Incorporate this into your morning rituals.

CLEANSE THIS SPACE WITCH'S POWDER

THE LORE

Another Cornish tradition was the use of working powder crafted by the Witch. These powders were used for an array of things to conjure their needs and desires. The Witch would either cast the powder onto themselves, another person, an item, or even an animal. The creation of this powder is a combination of cleansing herbs foraged from the local land with lore aligning with cleansing. Salt is often used when it comes to cleansing spells and holy rituals. In Scottish lore, salt was used to sprinkle around the butter churn in order to prevent the Witch from disrupting the butter, turning it sour. In some regions of England and Scotland, it was believed to be bad luck to offer someone salt due to the ties the salt has on the lender, in which curses could be casted upon them.

THE SPELL

This spell can be performed to cleanse out the old and reestablish wards and barriers from bewitchment and negativity.

A spoonful of salt

A spoonful of dried vervain

Frankincense resin

Mortar and pestle

Combine the salt, vervain, and frankincense resin into your mortar. State the incantation over the ingredients:

Spirit of Salt, I call upon you
to remove the old in this space.
Spirit of Vervain, I call upon you
to banish ill in this place.
Spirit of Frankincense, I call upon you
to omit the remains that linger.

With the pestle, grind these ingredients together, focusing on the energy between you, the pestle, and the herbs. As you grind, visualize these herbs coming to life. Speak with them about your desired outcome.

When it is ground into a fine powder, sprinkle it across your home starting from the back and working your way towards the front. Allow it to sit for a few moments, giving the spirits time to work their magic in cleansing your space.

Using your broom, sweep the powder away starting from the back. Collect the powder remnants and place them into the trash, removing the trash immediately from your space.

Spell Maintenance

This can be done for every New Moon for a consistent cleansing ritual for the Witch, or as frequently as the Witch desires.

Home Reset Floor Wash

The Lore

Tending to the home is something the Witch is familiar with, as it not only secures their magical workings, but it is also their safe space for their craft. Consistent cleanses were important to reassure their space was free from any stagnant or negative energy that would interfere with their everyday life and magical space. Among folk practices in the New World and beyond, the cleansing of the floors was a mundane-turned-magical act. Vinegar was often an important ingredient, as it was known to remove bacteria, and therefore removed negativity.

In England, a variation of a popular vinegar concoction can be found called the Four Thieves Vinegar. This medicine comes from many different traditions across Europe, varying in specifics but ultimately containing one commonality—vinegar. The lore of the recipe comes from four thieves who were scavenging the infected cities in France and England during the 1700s when the Great Plague spread through Europe. Once captured, they released the recipe in exchange for being released and kept safe. The recipe spread, where in England the lore granted its name, the Four Thieves Vinegar.

The Spell

Prior to washing your floors, brew this concoction to remove negativity and ill will:

6 lemons, sliced

1 tbsp / 15 ml of apple cider vinegar

A pinch of dried nettle

A spoonful of salt

3 cups / 720 ml of water, approximate

Combine the six sliced lemons, vinegar, pinch of dried nettle, and salt into a pot. Add about 3 cups (720 ml) of water. Simmer on the stovetop, brewing the concoction together for about 5 to 7 minutes. Remove from the stovetop and strain the ingredients into a separate bucket. (Note: if you decided on lemon essential oil instead of fresh lemons, add three drops here.)

Add about 1 tbsp/15 ml of the concoction to your floor wash to mop your home, working your way from the back of the home towards the front.

Spell Maintenance

To dispose of the water, pour it away from your home whether at a crossroads, or at the end of your street. If you're unable, simply pouring it down the drain works just fine. Give your sink a good rinse to reassure no remnants will linger.

CLEAR AWAY STAGNANCY CAULDRON BREW

The Lore

In Great Britain, common Juniper was found across the rolling hills and enchanted Scottish Highlands. In Scottish lore, it was said that in order to prevent the Plague from spreading, one would use the fumes of Juniper wood. Its earthy smell would repel the Plague and keep the community clean and healthy. In the Middle Ages, Juniper berries would be used to sweeten and flavor Scottish whiskey beverages. A tale from Buckinghamshire tells the story of Juniper bushes gossiping. Because of this and my personal experience with the Juniper plant, it is a great ally when clearing away stagnancy that prevents us from thinking and seeing clearly.

The Spell

To clear away stagnancy within the home, we will craft a concoction within our cauldron, or cast-iron skillet or stovetop pot.

Cast-iron skillet or stovetop pot

Handful of juniper berries, fresh or dried

3 cinnamon sticks

1 orange, sliced

Water

In the cast-iron skillet or pot, combine the juniper berries, cinnamon sticks, and orange slices. Add just enough water so that there is about an inch (2.5 cm) left at the top. Place the skillet on the stovetop over low heat. As it begins to simmer, state the incantation:

Cleanse away ill with this brew
Reset this place back anew

Allow it to simmer, keeping an eye on the water level to prevent the ingredients from burning.

Spell Maintenance

Perform this cauldron brew, or simmer pot, at the New Moon to cleanse away old, stagnant energy. The Witch may also decide to use this on a Sunday to refresh for the week ahead. To dispose of the brew, simply strain the water and safely dispose the ingredients. You may use the water as a wash for your doorways, windows, and baseboards for further deep cleansing. Dispose of the water down the drain.

Crafting Your Besom

The Lore

The besom, or broom, is often found as a hedge-crossing tool across the Witch's lore. It was also a common item found in the Witch's home for mundane cleaning activities to sweep away dirt within the home. To the Witch, it is more than that; it also serves as their instrument to fly between worlds. In Cornish traditions, it was believed that the act of sweeping could be of cleansing or cursing. Doorways are liminal spaces, and illness could be swept into this space to cause havoc to one's enemy. To bring about good fortune and abundance, one would use their right hand to sweep with the besom, while their left hand swept away negativity and harm. Your local region will inspire how you can go about crafting your own besom from the ground up. Each tree has their own stories and legends that speak of their magical correspondences.

OAK: strength, wisdom, power, protection against lightning

HAWTHORN: fertility, spiritual connection, new beginnings

PINE: healing, protection, empowerment

MOUNTAIN ASH, OR ROWAN: protection against bewitchment and ill-will, strength

WILLOW: healing, intuition, connection, love

The Spell

To craft one's tools is a chance to use our personal energy. The attention to detail and craftmanship enchants the tool to become empowered for magical intentions. If you choose to craft your own besom, follow the instructions below:

A stick from a local tree, preferably one you have a connection with—the width of the stick should be sturdy. The length is up to your personal preference. Choose a stick that has already naturally fallen from the tree.

Foraged natural elements such as twigs, branches with leaves, etc.

Glue, optional

Cord

Begin by laying the stick on the ground. Take the twigs and other foraged material like leaves and lay them around the end of the stick, creating a bushel. You may decide to glue the twigs to this end to help hold it in place. Take the cord and tie the straw around the end of the stick until it is secure in place. Tie a knot to set the cord in place.

An alternative to crafting your own besom is purchasing one during the autumnal season. You can find the popular cinnamon brooms at your local grocery store around September. These are a great alternative to handcrafting your own. They are crafted from all-natural materials, and dipped in a cinnamon-scented perfume to fill your space with the warm aroma.

To enchant the besom for protection and to aid in spirit-flight, you will need:

A cauldron or fire-safe container   **Frankincense resin**

A charcoal disk   **A spoonful of mugwort**

In your cauldron or fire-safe container, light the charcoal disk. Place the frankincense resin and pinch of mugwort to burn. As the fumes rise, place your besom over it and state the incantation thrice:

Enchanted with my will and desire,
may this besom take my spirit higher.
By straw and wood,
The besom's aid is understood.

To use in spirit-flight, place the besom underneath your knees prior to a flight session. Allow it to "lift" you off into the Otherworld.

Spell Maintenance

Place the besom near your altar space as a protection ward when not in use for flight. You may decide to add other natural elements to it, such as flowers and greenery. Adding such elements complements the already enchanted item with additional energies. For added protection, decorate it with mistletoe or rosemary. For healing and intuition, decorate it with rose or sunflowers. To enchant the item after some time, reinstate the incantation above over the incense blend. If you decide to relocate to a new home, discard the besom. In Irish lore it is bad luck to bring along an old besom, as it holds the energies of the old space.

See image on page 112.

Home Blessing Cornbread

The Lore

Across Great Britain, it was a common tradition to greet a new neighbor with homemade loaves, coal, and even coins. This was to bring forth good luck and prosperity for the new home. Salt was held in high regard across Great Britain. In the Scottish Highlands, salt was so powerful that any food, like bread, that left one's home would be sprinkled with it to prevent the Faefolk from taking it away as a treat. There are undoubtedly countless traditions that honor the goodness of bread, ranging from religious ceremonies and beliefs. Every tradition, religion, and culture has their own lore and ways about bringing bread into their traditions, but most agree that it is a sacred offering to spirits or among neighbors. In the Appalachian Mountains, cornbread was a common dish on the dinner table. A true American staple item, if I dare say. I found this cornbread to be one of my favorite items when visiting family. Someone always brought a dish of it, and if I was lucky there would be several.

The Spell

To bless a home, bake this homemade cornbread as an offering to the house spirit. This can also be made for a new neighbor or family member as a token of abundance and prosperity ahead.

1 tbsp / 15 g butter

A cast-iron skillet, seasoned

1 cup / 122 g of yellow ground cornmeal

1 tsp / 6 g of salt

¾ cup / 94 g of all-purpose flour

¼ cup / 50 g of granulated sugar

½ tsp of baking soda

2 tsp / 9 g of baking powder

⅓ cup / 80 ml of whole milk

8 tbsp / 120 ml of unsalted, melted butter

2 eggs

Salt, for sprinkling

Preheat the oven to 400° F (200° C). Coat the cast-iron skillet with butter. In a bowl, combine the cornmeal, salt, flour, sugar, baking soda, and baking powder. Mix well. Then, create a crater in the center of the mixture to add the whole milk, melted butter, and eggs. Mix well, until it is a smooth consistency. As you begin mixing, speak the incantation:

With goodness in my heart,
protect this home from tearing apart.
A roof over our head, food on the table,
let this home be nothing but stable.

Pour the batter into the skillet as evenly as possible. Place the skillet into the oven for about 20 minutes, or until the top is brown and the center is well done.

Consume the cornbread among good people. Sharing a meal that is blessed among those you love and admire amplifies the energy of the spell. Enjoy it at your altar or at the dinner table, or simply send it off to its new home. But don't forget to sprinkle a little salt on top to prevent the Faefolk from stealing it under your nose as you leave the house!

Cleanse the Old Self Ritual

The Lore

There is a time and place for when we want to express gratitude for older versions of ourselves that allowed us to remain safe during a chapter of our lives. Although past patterns and beliefs can no longer come with us into a new chapter, we can still remember who we were. In some ways, this is a funeral for these older versions of ourselves. In many traditions, funerals are a very serious matter. You see it in shows, movies, and old lore—there are an array of funeral traditions dependent on culture and religious customs. In this case, we will be inspired by our personal journey thus far.

The Spell

Before performing the ritual, begin by creating the following cleansing scrub.

A handful of salt

A spoonful of dried rosemary

A spoonful of dried vervain

A spoonful of dried rose petals

1 tbsp / 15 ml of olive oil, or other carrier oil of your choice, free from allergic reactions

Combine the salt, rosemary, vervain, and rose petals into a bowl. Add the olive oil, mixing well. You should have a scrub-like consistency.

To begin the ritual, you will need access to the following:

A shower or bathtub

4 white tealight candles

Charcoal disk

Cauldron for burning frankincense resin

Frankincense resin

A cup of your favorite beverage—this can be alcoholic or not—something that you really enjoy and is considered a treat for yourself.

A second cup left empty

Cleanse the bathroom how you see fit, either with smoke, your energy, or a sound like a bell. With the Cleansing Scrub, wash your entire body and rinse thoroughly.

After your cleansing shower, you will need to find a quiet space for the remainder of the ritual. This can be in your bedroom, a safe space outdoors, or wherever you feel safest. Take yourself here along with four white tealight candles—one to represent each of the elements.

Sit in this quiet space that you feel most comfortable. Place the four tealight candles around you—one in front, one to the left, one behind, and the last to the right. Light them each, starting with the one to the left in a clockwise direction. With your cauldron in front of you, light a charcoal disk. Add frankincense resin to burn, allowing the fumes to rise. As the fumes rise, our words rise to the Otherworld for spirits to hear.

In many funeral traditions, there was a toast or speech to the one who passed. In this ritual, we adopt the same tradition but to our past self. It is always nice to salute and express gratitude to our past selves for doing what they knew best at the time with the knowledge and experience they had. Here are some moments to consider in your toast:

Recall a moment where your past self kept you safe

Recall a moment where your past self made you proud

Recall a moment where your past self experienced joy

Recall a moment where your past self learned something new

As you toast to yourself, raise your glass of chosen favorite beverage. Once you are finished, pour just a bit into a separate cup and take a sip yourself. A salute to the past you.

Spell Maintenance

You may finish the remaining liquid or dispose of it. Use the Cleansing Scrub anytime you are in need of a spiritual cleanse. It is a great addition for spiritual hygiene and to incorporate into your routine.

See image on page 70.

CHAPTER 6
FOR PROTECTION

The other aspect when it comes to maintaining a spiritual hygiene routine is protection. After we have taken the initiative to cleanse away old, stagnant, or unwanted energy, we then want to ensure that our space and ourselves are protected. In some cases, when we are traveling or going about our everyday, we can take along with us added protective energy. When looking back at the history of the Witch, much of the folk magic and practices were indeed to interfere with bewitchment. Many would say that it wasn't magic at all, but instead a way to repel the Witch's curse. Today, the Witch who has created a craft using the folk customs of their ancestors may discover some personal protection remedies specific to their culture. These ways are passed down for a reason and continue to be used today, and that is because they work. The spells shared here are inspired by folk ways and magic that can be used in today's modern world to protect ourselves from any outside energy. Let them be an inspiration in protecting your peace, spirit, and space.

THE WITCH'S BOTTLE

THE LORE

Archaeologists discovered what is referred to as the Witch's bottle in the seventeenth century across England. These bottles were found within the flooring of homes. The bottles themselves were either crafted from stoneware or glassware, protecting the ingredients inside, including nails or pins, hair, and even fingernails. It was believed that this would be used as a decoy for any bewitchment cast upon them, a form of protection. The home of the Witch wasn't the only place these bottles would be stored away. The grounds of churches, the hearth of homes, and even riverbanks were special locations to store these protection bottles away. In 1976, a similar bottle was discovered in Delaware that provided insight into the witchery performed in the late eighteenth century here in North America. Containing six pins, urine, and a broken bird bone, the suspicion was that this particular bottle, found on the land belonging to settlers by the name of Taylor, was placed near the home of their previous ancestors in the early 1700s as a form of sympathetic magic to cure illness.

THE SPELL

For a modernized version of the Witch's bottle, we may decide to remove urine, fingernails, and hair and instead replace them with corresponding herbs. Though there is something to say about the folk ways of the Witch, it is entirely up to the Witch today to decide whether they want to use bodily fluids and products.

Black candle

Glass bottle or stone jar with lid, any size

Piece of parchment paper

A pen

3 thorns from a Hawthorn tree

A spoonful of salt

A spoonful of cayenne pepper

3 sprigs of rosemary

Clipping of your own hair or fingernails (or both), optional

White vinegar

Material Substitutions

If you're uncomfortable utilizing a talisman such as hair or fingernails, you can use an item that belongs to you such as a piece of fabric from an article of clothing. The purpose of it being something that has your energy that can be used as a decoy.

Center and ground your energy. Light a black candle to focus your energy on banishing negativity. At this time, you may call upon other spirit allies, if you wish. To begin, cleanse a glass or stone jar. With the parchment paper, write the petition:

Capture and destroy baneful energy caught inside this vessel.

Roll the petition away from you and place it in the glass bottle or jar with lid.

To follow, add the three thorns, salt, cayenne pepper, and rosemary, addressing each ingredient's purpose in this spell.

Hawthorn, capture the harm.
Cayenne pepper, destroy the harm.
Salt, cleanse the harm.
Rosemary, protect me from harm.

Lastly, take a clipping of your own hair or fingernails (or another personal item as discussed above) to use as a talisman and add it to the bottle. Fill the bottle with vinegar. Close the bottle.

To seal the bottle, pour the wax from the black candle over the top, sealing all the ingredients inside. Enchant the bottle by shaking it, visualizing all the ill will being directed into the bottle and being destroyed. Once charged, place the bottle in a safe space.

Spell Maintenance

To maintain your witch bottle, shake it at least once a week to recharge it with energy, visualizing all the ill-will being sent into the jar and destroyed. Every new moon, replace it with a new bottle. Carefully remove the wax from the top and pour the ingredients into the trash. Because we are using salt in this bottle, it is not safe to return to the Earth, as it is not good for grass. Dispose of the trash away from your home. Cleanse the bottle with either smoke, your energy, or the sound from a bell. Then, work through the steps again.

See image on page 128.

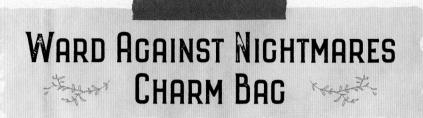

Ward Against Nightmares Charm Bag

The Lore

The star anise is a spice that found its way to Europe from China in the 1500s. It was commonly used in teas and food dishes all over the world. Today, the Witch may use this spice during the festive winter seasons, as it helps provide warmth during the cooler days in hot teas. It is also quite decorative and can be used as a charm ornament on the Yule tree.

The Spell

Whenever you need protection against nightmares for a good night's rest, this charm bag can be used.

A cloth bag

White tea light

A spoonful of lavender

A sprig of rosemary

A spoonful of dried valerian

3 star anise pods

A pen

Petition paper

Gather your ingredients together at your altar space. Mindfully add the lavender, rosemary, valerian, and anise pods into the cloth bag.

Onto your petition paper, write the incantation:

Tonight, I banish what hinders my sleep
from any scares that decide to creep.
Lavender, rosemary, valerian, and anise,
help me keep my peace.

Fold the paper three times. Place the folded incantation into the cloth bag. Enchant the cloth bag by lighting the white tea light candle and placing it on top of the cloth bag. Spend a few breaths here, focusing your gaze on the white light. Then, extinguish the light and set it aside. You may place the cloth bag underneath your pillow for a peaceful sleep or hang it above your bed.

Spell Maintenance

To dispose of the spell, remove the contents from the cloth bag. Burn the piece of paper along with the dried lavender and valerian, then dispose of the ashes. You may cleanse and use the star anise pods for another spell. Cleanse the cloth bag before using for another charm.

Ward Against Unwanted Visitors Charm Wreath

The Lore

When it comes to warding the home, there are many materials we can use. Protecting the home and their property was highly important to the Witch and common folks. There are an array of tales of plants corresponding to warding the home, such as Rowan, Ash, and Bay. A Cornish tradition found that using Bay protected the cattle from getting sick. If the keeper felt their cattle was undergoing some illness, they would craft a wreath with Bay and its leaves, placing it around the cattle's neck for good health. Rowan is also a tree that was used to ward against bewitchment and evil. The Rowan Cross was a charm found in Britain using two twigs from the Rowan tree, tied together to make a cross with red thread.

The Spell

To ward our home against illness, bewitchment, bad luck, and negativity, we will craft a wreath to place on our front door. This is a great way to connect with your local surroundings, incorporating the natural cycles of your neighboring plant allies into your home.

Foraged leaves and sticks from local plants

3 garlic heads, optional

In-season flowers

Undecorated wreath

Floral wire

Forage fallen leaves and sticks from local tree allies that correspond to protection such as bay, hawthorn, rowan, and elder. The connection to your local land and neighborhood will be the most important resource when it comes to deciphering which trees you have connected with for this spell. Grab quite the bundle to cover the wreath.

If you're able, gather three heads of garlic as well. Garlic is most known for its protection against vampires—but whether vampires are real or not, garlic is great to ward away any negativity and illness. Medicinally, garlic is an aid for the immune system and can fight off unwanted bacteria.

Next, look to your local farmers market for in-season flowers. For protection, consider flowers with thorns, like roses. Roses are most known for their language of love, but they are often used to ward off anyone with ill intentions, too. Feel free to visit your local grocery store if your local market does not have any roses.

Together, you will have a bundle of natural accents with which to decorate a wreath from your local craft store. Begin by tying the tree branches and twigs that you foraged around the wreath in a clockwise direction using floral wire to secure them in place. Do this until the wreath is fully covered. Next, with the roses, integrate them into the wreath bundle, using your intuition to decipher their placement along with any other flowers you chose.

If you managed to find some garlic heads, you may tie them to the wreath from the top center so that they hang down, or you may also integrate them into the wreath.

Once you have crafted your wreath, state the incantation as you hold it:

May this bundle bless this space,
warding against bewitchment of this place.
A home filled with peace and kind,
no illness will ever mind.
So long this bundle is set here,
all evil spirits will forever fear.

Place the wreath on your front door.

Spell Maintenance

Refresh the wreath in every season. Return the natural elements back to the Earth as necessary, expressing gratitude for their energy and warding.

*See image on page 36.

Protect Me Anointing Oil

The Lore

Yarrow, or *Achillea millefolium*, was also referred to as the Devil's Nettle due to its association with the Devil. Because of this, many believed it to be a plant that belonged to the Witch. Yarrow was used to avert curses and hexes casted by the Witch and was also used in divination methods. Witches aside, it was also known as the military herb, aiding Achilles in healing battle wounds, as taught by his mentor, Chiron. But as we take a closer look at the plant, we recognize that its characteristics align with its medicinal capabilities to heal cuts and wounds. Spend some time with Yarrow, and you will undoubtedly feel its healing and protective energy.

The Spell

This anointing oil can be used to anoint yourself, divination tools, tools used in your craft, and thresholds.

An empty tincture bottle with a dropper, any size

Pinch of dried yarrow (You can use the entire plant: stem, flowers, and leaves.)

6 whole cloves

3 bay leaves

Olive oil, or yarrow-infused oil

Gather your ingredients. Cleanse the bottle either with smoke, your energy, or a sound like a bell. Place the dried yarrow, whole cloves, and bay leaves into the bottle. Then, pour the olive oil into the bottle with the herbs and fill until it is full. Close the bottle with the top dropper. Enchant the item by shaking the bottle, focusing on waking up the ingredients inside.

Spell Maintenance

Keep the anointment oil in a cool, dry, dark area. It will keep for up to a year. When empty, wash the tincture bottle and cleanse to reuse for another oil.

Protect These Walls Candle

The Lore

There are some prayers and enchanted words that have survived many generations. They are often of the prominent language spoken then, such as Latin. One of the most popular historic prayers among folk practitioners is the SATOR Square charm. The origins of this charm are still debated between historians and archaeologists, whether it is an old Latin prayer from the Christian church or even older than that. This ward was used in

S	A	T	O	R
A	R	E	P	O
T	E	N	E	T
O	P	E	R	A
R	O	T	A	S

the thresholds of the home to protect against bewitchment and illness, often written on a piece of paper and placed into a doorframe to capture the illness before entering the home.

The Spell

This spell will repel any unwanted energy within the space.

A cast-iron skillet

Piece of paper

Pen

A black candle

Protect Me Anointing Oil
(see page 137)

Cleanse This Space Witch's Powder
(see page 116)

Place the cast-iron skillet on a flat surface. With the piece of paper and pen, draw the SATOR Square, illustrated above. Place this on the center of the skillet.

Wake up the black candle by rubbing it between your hands. Dress the black candle with three drops of the Protect Me Anointing Oil. Place the black candle in a candle holder or light the bottom of the candle to soften the end so that it is securely on top of the piece of paper with the SATOR Square.

Using the Cleanse This Space Witch's Powder, sprinkle a circle around the candle and SATOR Square paper. As you light the candle, state the incantation:

I banish away the ill behind each wall,
the ugly and cursed be exiled and fall.

A shield of armor casted around this place,
may no negative energy leave a trace.

Allow the candle to burn all the way down. Once the candle is done, remove the remnants of the candle. Fold the SATOR Square paper and place it in a threshold of your home.

Spell Maintenance

This ward can be reaffirmed every New Moon. Remove the old SATOR Square and burn it, returning the ashes somewhere along your property.

Enchanted
Ancestor Charms

The Lore

Prayers beads are often found across different religions and customs. They allow the practitioner to focus on their spoken words reaching to their beloved spirits. The intention and focus on these beads during prayer allows the practitioner to enter a trance-like state where connection between them and their spirits are reached. It is a sacred tool that strengthens their focus and is used exclusively for spiritual connection.

The Spell

When crafting prayer beads, you can use different symbolisms and charms to create something unique for your ancestors. You may choose to use these beads during moments of conversation with your ancestors or other spirits.

Cord measuring the length of which you would like the beads to be— consider a certain number of beads in increments of the sacred three (3, 6, 9, 12 . . .)

Any color and selection of beads you would like to use

Charms selected by you to represent your ancestors or other spirits— consider their hobbies, favorite places, animals, etc. for inspiration

Begin by gathering your materials at your altar. Tie a knot at the bottom of the cord to hold the beads. As you place the beads onto the cord, speak to your spirits or ancestors, telling them what you are doing and what these will be used for. When inserting a charm, state the intention behind this charm. Why did you choose it? What did it resemble to you? What intention do you have behind it? For example, you may choose a key to represent unlocked skills or opportunities that your spirits or ancestors may assist you with.

Add your beads and charms until the string is complete. Tie a knot at the top when you are finished.

To enchant this item, you will need:

Ancestor Connection Incense Blend
(see page 53)

Charcoal disk

Cauldron or fire-safe container

Burn the Ancestor Connection Incense Blend on the charcoal disk. As the smoke rises, allow the fumes to enchant the beads. Speak out loud to your ancestral spirits the purpose of these beads:

> *I, (your name), enchant these beads to be a tether between you and me.*
> *When I speak to you with these in my hand, hear my spoken words.*
> *They will rise and reach you.*

SPELL MAINTENANCE

Keep this charm near your ancestor's altar or carry them along with you for spiritual connection.

Hag Stone Charm

The Lore

Hag stones found at the shore are a physical representation of the Otherworldly magic between the sea and earth. Hag stones, which are also referred to as fairy stones with their connection to the Otherworld, were used for protection workings in Britain. They are a stone with a natural-formed hole created by the power of the ocean. Often one would tie a cord through the hole, incorporating knot magic by tying a significant number of knots into the cord. An intention was stated into the knots for a desired outcome. As red thread was commonly used in folk magic for protection, one would incorporate a red thread with the hag stone for such intentions.

The Spell

To protect yourself or your space, seek out a hag stone at your local beachside. They are most commonly found around the coastline, with the waves having enough force to form the hole within the stone. If you are not local to a coastline, you may source them from online shops.

A 6-inch / 15-cm long piece of red thread or yarn

One hag stone

Dragon's blood resin or incense

Fire-safe container or cauldron, if using resin

Charcoal disk, if using incense

Feed the red thread through the hole of the hag stone. Tie three knots at the top, stating your intention for protection.

Hold the hag stone with red thread above the lit incense or resin in your burning cauldron. Allow the smoke to fumigate the charm to enchant it with the magic of protection. As you hold it, speak a prayer or incantation such as the following:

Enchanted this item will be, protecting from woes and negativity.

Spell Maintenance

Place this on a door in your home to protect your space, in your vehicle to protect you during travels, or carry it with you for self-protection. To re-enchant this charm for every Full Moon, state the incantation over frankincense or dragon's blood incense.

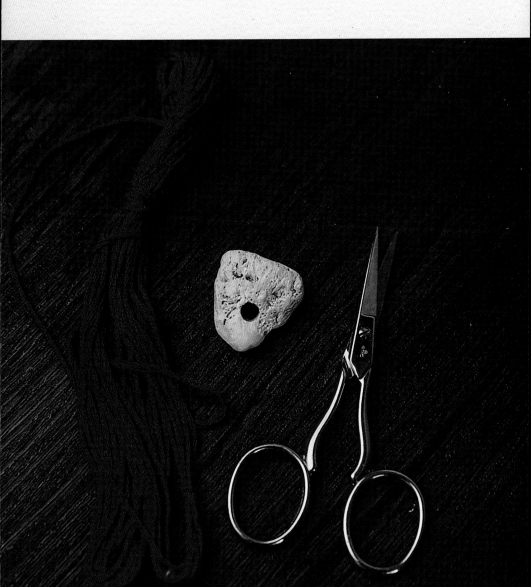

CHAPTER 7
FOR HEALING

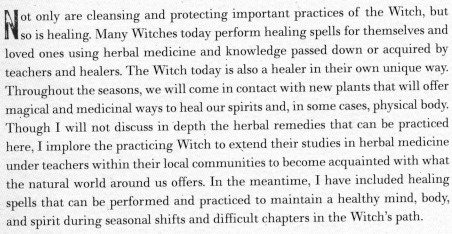

Not only are cleansing and protecting important practices of the Witch, but so is healing. Many Witches today perform healing spells for themselves and loved ones using herbal medicine and knowledge passed down or acquired by teachers and healers. The Witch today is also a healer in their own unique way. Throughout the seasons, we will come in contact with new plants that will offer magical and medicinal ways to heal our spirits and, in some cases, physical body. Though I will not discuss in depth the herbal remedies that can be practiced here, I implore the practicing Witch to extend their studies in herbal medicine under teachers within their local communities to become acquainted with what the natural world around us offers. In the meantime, I have included healing spells that can be performed and practiced to maintain a healthy mind, body, and spirit during seasonal shifts and difficult chapters in the Witch's path.

A Witch's Traditional Fire Cider

The Lore

This oxymel is a common herbal remedy when it comes to herbal medicine. Though it is an old remedy, it became popular by herbalist and founder of the California School of Herbal Studies, Rosemary Gladstar, in the 1970s. The term oxymel stems from the Greek word *oxymeli*, meaning acid and honey. This concoction is just that and is fruitful for fighting off bacteria that develops into a common cold. The "fire" piece comes from the ingredients used in this tonic and often warms the body during the cooler months of the year. This is where herbal medicine and magic collide. By using plant allies and our connection to our bioregion, we discover answers to heal our bodies and protect them during the winter months.

The Spell

For this tincture, you will need:

A 32-oz / 907-g mason jar

1 large red onion, chopped

2 heads of garlic, chopped

½ cup / 48 g of grated ginger

½ cup / 48 g of grated turmeric root

¼ cup / 37 g of diced jalapeño

2 lemons, sliced

¼ cup / 10 g of fresh thyme

Organic apple cider vinegar

Parchment paper

Honey, optional

In the clean mason jar, add the red onion, garlic, ginger, turmeric, jalapeños, lemon, and thyme. Fill the jar to the top with the organic apple cider vinegar. Place some parchment paper on top then seal with the lid.

Place this concoction in a safe place to steep for about 3 to 4 weeks. Once ready, strain the ingredients, returning them to the Earth with gratitude. Add some warm honey to taste. Take a spoonful when you feel like you are coming down with a cold. (Note: Always inquire with a certified physican or herbalist before taking this and other herbal supplements.)

Spell Maintenance

Store in your medicine cabinet, or in the refrigerator, where it can be used within six months.

HEAL MY HEART ANOINTING OIL

THE LORE

Motherwort was a sacred herb that was used as a tea for pregnant people to relief stress and anxiety. Across Europe, it was believed it could cure cattle diseases. In the Victorian Language of Flowers, motherwort spoke on a concealed love. Its symbolism with matters of the heart tells us that this plant ally can do magic in times of heartache and is a support in times of need.

THE SPELL

This spell may be performed on Friday in correspondence with Venus day. For this anointment oil, you will need:

An empty tincture bottle (any size is fine), with a dropper

A spoonful of dried motherwort

A spoonful of dried roses

Your carrier oil of choice; my personal favorite for anything on the skin is either olive oil or fractionated coconut oil, for their long shelf life

Spiritually cleanse the empty tincture bottle. Place the dried motherwort and roses into the container, topping it off with your carrier oil of choice. Close the bottle with the lid and shake it awake. As you shake, speak the incantation:

Motherwort, I ask of you
to relieve the heartache that makes me blue.
Rose, I seek to you
to protect my heart from harm others do.

Use this anointment oil on yourself during times of need, or on other tools for other healing spells.

SPELL MAINTENANCE

This anointment oil can be kept in a cool, dry area such as your altar. Prior to use, shake it awake and state the incantation to infuse the ingredients with new energy.

See image on page 144.

Rooted in Gratitude Ritual

The Lore

The Witch remains grounded, and nature is an accompanying friend in this practice. One of the many things I learned during my own healing journey was how important it is to root yourself in gratitude. We get caught up in our daily, rushed life so easily in a world that requires us to constantly move about. Spending time to slow down, take a breath, and remember how far we have gotten is a practice that allows us to reflect. When you think back on the previous month, three months, or even a year, are you able to list all the things you've accomplished? Or how things you wished are now present in your life? With this ritual, we will root ourselves in gratitude.

The Spell

For this ritual, you will need a Gratitude Potion for the morning.

About 1 tbsp / 8 g of dried orange peel

About ½ tbsp / 4 g of dried lemongrass

About ½ tbsp / 4 g of licorice root

Combine the orange peel, lemongrass, and licorice root together in a small bowl. Then add to a steeping teapot for about 3 to 4 minutes. Pour yourself a cup first thing in the morning.

Go outside on a fresh, early morning with your Gratitude Potion in hand and enjoy mindfully.

Spend some time walking in the grass, focusing on the feeling of the Earth beneath your feet. As the Sun begins to peak upon the horizon, open yourself by raising your hands up high. Take a deep breath in, then out. Do this three times. As the Sun rises, speak out five things you are grateful for. This can be anything that comes to mind from the heart. Tell them to the Sun. Allow the gratitude to warm your heart and fill your spirit. Lastly, give thanks to the Sun's light and energy for the day ahead.

See image on page 3.

Support My Physical and Spiritual Heart Spell

The Lore

Hawthorn trees are also known as the Witch's tree. Its relationship with the Otherworld is spoken about across Europe. Its stories tie it with the Faefolk. It was believed to be bad luck to bring a hawthorn tree branch into your home unless it was on the celebratory folkloric fire festival celebrated across Great Britain and Ireland on the first of May. During the spring seasons, the tree has blossoms that smell delightful and are believed to lure people to rest underneath in order to be kidnapped by the Faefolk and dragged into the Otherworld. There are many medicinal benefits to this magical tree, as it is one that aids in cardiovascular health. Using the haws that blossom during the wintery months that are bright red, an herbalist may craft a tincture for their apothecary.

The Spell

For this spell, you will need:

A white candle

A carving tool

Candle holder

Heal My Heart Anointment Oil
(from page 148)

3 thorns from the hawthorn tree

A cord of red thread about the
circumference of your left wrist,
allowing it to be a little loose to
accommodate the haws

9 haws from a hawthorn tree

A sewing needle

Gather your materials at your altar. To begin, take the white candle and carve your name and birthdate into it. Tap the candle awake or rub it in between your hands. Place the white candle in a candle holder. Anoint the candle with the Heal My Heart Anointment Oil.

Take the thorns foraged from the hawthorn tree and place them around the candle. Lay the red thread around the candle, and place the haws outside the thread. As you light the candle, state the incantation:

Spirit of the Hawthorn,
I call to you here and now,
enchant these tools with your gift,
any ache and pain, you will lift.

Allow the candle to burn for a few moments. Extinguish the candle and remove the cord and haws. Thread the cord into the sewing needle. Tie a knot at the end. Then add the haws to the cord. Once complete, tie the cord around your left wrist. This hand is tied to the heart. Wear this charm for three days to strengthen your heart spiritually.

Spell Maintenance

To dispose of the charm after three days, cut the charm off your wrist. Return the haws back to the Earth, giving thanks. Dispose of the cord into the trash.

Walk in the Present Ritual

The Lore

It is not uncommon to feel discouraged sometimes about where we are in life. When walking the Witch's path, there are moments in which we question whether or not we are meant to be where we are presently. Sometimes we wonder if we should be more "ahead," while other times we tend to remain in the past. Our human minds like to wander off, comparing our path to someone else's. Honor where you are in this present moment. Express gratitude for how far you've already come. This ritual is to aid your spirit and mind within the present.

The Spell

For this ritual, you will need a Present Moment Anointment Oil.

An empty tincture bottle (any size), with a dropper

Carrier oil of your choice, such as olive oil or fractionated coconut oil

A spoonful of valerian for peace

A spoonful of peppermint for focus

Gather your materials at your altar. Cleanse the empty tincture jar. Add the carrier oil of your choosing, something that is easy on the skin. Add the dried ingredients of valerian and peppermint. Close the bottle and shake the ingredients awake.

Take this anointment oil with you on a morning walk to your favorite place. This can be a local park, a river, or anywhere you feel at peace. Find a quiet spot here. Sit in a comfortable position and allow your spirit to connect with the spirits here. Introduce yourself to the surrounding local spirits (refer to page 30), telling them that you are here to root yourself in the present. They may greet you or simply leave you be.

Once you are settled and comfortable, focus your attention on your spirit, the inner knowing. Allow your shoulders to drop and thoughts to come and go. Place some of the anointment oil in your hand and rub them together. Then, anoint your feet. Place your feet on the ground. Visualize them taking root here, stabilizing your spirit in the present moment. As you visualize taking root in the present, chant the incantation:

> *In this moment, I am here.*
> *I am present, my mind clear.*
> *There is nowhere else I need to be.*
> *In this moment, my spirit is free.*

As you visualize your feet taking root and your spirit releasing any worries or responsibilities in this exact moment, allow your physical body to relax. Be as present as possible, removing external factors for just this moment. Focus on your breathing, reciting the incantation as needed.

After a few moments, when you are feeling fulfilled and your intuition calls for your spirit to return, express gratitude. Gratitude is a practice that can root us in times of worry and discouragement. Thank the local spirits for their presence and return home.

Spell Maintenance

Take anything that you brought with you back, leaving no trace behind.

Bid My Worries Away Spell

The Lore

Cornflower was thought to have been a gift from the sky with its vibrant hues. Its Latin name, *centaurea cyanus*, was said to have derived from the Greek mythological figure, Chiron. Chiron was known for his knowledge of healing herbal medicine. Hence, the flower's association with healing remedies. In the nineteenth century, this flower was used as buttons to be worn on jackets as a divination tool for the wearer's love life. If the flower wilted and died quickly it was believed that their beloved chosen person would not return their love.

The Spell

For this spell, you will need:

A piece of paper

A pen

A lighter

Fire-safe cauldron

A mortar and pestle

A handful of dried cornflowers

To begin, take the piece of paper and pen to write down your current worry. Write as much or as little as you'd like, but be as specific as you can. Fold the paper three times away from you. Using the lighter, ignite this and place it into your cauldron. Allow it to burn to ashes.

Place the ashes into the mortar and pestle. Take the handful of dried cornflowers and add them into the mortar and pestle. As you grind them together, state the incantation:

Fear not, my worrywart
with comfort and loving support,
these thoughts leave my mind
and replaced with things that are kind.

Once you have ground these together into a fine powder, take it with you outside on a windy day. Visualize the worry that you had written on the piece of paper. Then pour the powder into your hand to blow the powder away from you, into the wind. Allow the wind to take it away from you and disappear.

Spell Maintenance

Incorporate this spell into other New Moon rituals to be rid of old, stagnant energy, and to welcome new beginnings.

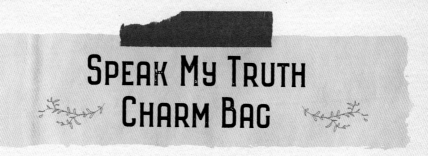

Speak My Truth Charm Bag

The Lore

Basil is a beloved plant that extends its reach far and beyond around the world. Its lore varies from blessing people with good fortune, to a symbolism of hate that later turned into love, and a powerful ward against evil spirits, and especially scorpions. The Romans utilized this powerful warding plant against their enemies, cursing them with ill intent. In England in the 1600s, basil was used medicinally by smelling it to help clear the sinuses and mind of those who had fallen ill. The lore behind this plant also spoke to how it was often used to unionize families and lovers after fights. Using a recipe that included basil would help soothe everyone, calming their frustrations and encouraging them to be kind to one another once again.

The Spell

For this spell, you will need:

A piece of paper

A pen

A cloth bag

A spoonful of dried basil

A spoonful of lavender

Gather your ingredients at your altar. With the piece of paper and pen, write down the petition: I speak my truth without fear and worry. Fold this piece of paper three times toward you. Place the petition inside the cloth bag, with the dried basil and lavender. Close the cloth bag. Rub the ingredients inside the bag, awakening the energy of its contents. As you do so, state the incantation:

My words are spoken without quiver,
no matter what situation, I will not shiver.
Truth is said without a doubt,
What I have to say others will hear about.

Carry this charm bag with you for important and difficult conversations. When we are on our healing journey, often we are met with a desire to speak on our needs and feelings. This can be with loved ones, friends, and other individuals such as therapists who are helping us on our journey. Rub this charm bag when you need extra confidence to speak your truth.

Spell Maintenance

To dispel this bag, remove the dried basil and lavender and return them into the Earth, expressing gratitude. Burn the petition in your cauldron and sprinkle the ashes somewhere on your property. Cleanse the cloth bag to be used in other workings.

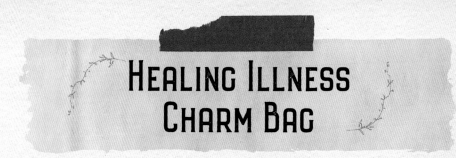

Healing Illness Charm Bag

The Lore

Charm bags were often found in folk traditions for healing and protection. Often crafted from old cloth, the bag would encompass magical herbs and written charms to be worn over the neck by the individual in need of healing. In British lore, St. John's Wort was a magical herb that assisted with protection against bewitchment and illness. The Gaelic incantation translated into English by Alexander Carmichael (1832–1912) speaks of this plant ally:

> *St. John's wort, St. John's wort,*
> *my envy whoever has thee,*
>
> *I will pluck thee with my right hand,*
> *I will preserve thee with my left hand,*
> *Whoso findeth thee in the cattle field,*
>
> *Shall never be without kine.*

With its powerful history and association with holy rituals and sacred healing energies, this plant can aid us in healing illness when combined with a written charm that has also been used to protect individuals' health. The ABRACADABRA written charm is most commonly found across Europe. Written on a petition paper and worn by the sick, the charm can cast away illness.

The Spell

For this spell, we will be combining the ABRACADABRA charm and the magical plant ally, St. John's wort, to craft our own healing charm bag against sickness.

A cloth bag	**A spoonful of St. John's wort**
Paper and pen	**A spoonful of yarrow**

Collect your material at your altar. Cleanse the cloth bag and set aside. With your pen and paper, write down the ABRACADABRA charm as such, dropping a letter by each line:

ABRACADABRA

ABRACADABR

ABRACADAB

ABRACADA

ABRACAD

ABRACA

ABRAC

ABRA

ABR

AB

A

Place the written charm into the cloth bag, followed by the St. John's wort and yarrow. Hold the charm bag in your hands, visualizing the healing energy of this charm throughout your physical body and spirit. Carry it with you for at least three days.

Spell Maintenance

After three days, remove the remnants of the cloth bag. Burn the healing charm paper, St. John's wort, and yarrow together in a fire-safe container, giving thanks to the spirits. Spiritually cleanse the cloth bag with smoke or your own energy to use for another spell.

Closing Thoughts
Seeing is Believing

Dear Reader, we have come to an end in our shared journey together. It is hard to believe it is already that time. If there is anything that I can leave you with, it is this bit of wisdom that I have learned along my personal journey: Seeing is believing. The more you put into practice, the more you will craft your unique magical path. With every one spell that worked, there will be a handful that didn't. It is a craft—a learning experience. A practice that will encourage you to move in ways that you have not before, getting creative with what's available, and inviting you to deep self-exploration. Your experiences will construct a craft that fits uniquely to you. There is a plethora of knowledge shared in this book to provide you with the tools and inspiration to further form your own magical path. But no matter the tool you craft, the spirit you conjure, or the spell you manifest, the most important tool is you. Personal empowerment may seem daunting, but consider the Witches before us that took matters into their hands for the necessity of protection against all odds. You are filled with as much magic as the trees, rivers, mountains, and oceans. My hope is that you recognize that and harness that energy to be the guide along your path. There may be moments that leave you questioning which street to take on the fork in the road. Listen to your spirit and trust that it will lead you in the right direction, no matter how treacherous things may appear.

Resources

The following books and online resources were collected for this book. The Witch may extend further research with the following sources.

Books

The 5 Love Languages by Gary Chapman

Animism: Respecting the Living World by Graham Harvey

An ABC of Witchcraft: Past and Present by Doreen Valiente, pp. 151

Botanical Folk Tales of Britain and Ireland by Lisa Schneidau

The Book of English Magic by Philip Carr-Gomm and Richard Heygate

A Brief History of Witchcraft by Lois Martin

A Broom at Midnight: 13 Gates of Witchcraft by Spirit Flight by Roger J. Horne

The Black Book of Isobel Gowdie: And Other Scottish Spells & Charms by Ash William Mills

The Black Toad: West Country Witchcraft and Magic by Gemma Gary

The Crooked Path: An Introduction to Traditional Witchcraft by Kelden, pp. 62

The Cunning Man's Handbook: The Practice of English Folk Magic 1550-1900 by Jim Baker

Folk Medicine in Southern Appalachia by Anthony Cavendar

The Gaelic Otherworld: John Gregorson Campbell's Superstitions of the Highlands and the Islands of Scotland and Witchcraft and Second Sight in the Highlands and Islands, edited by Ronald Black

The Horned God of the Witches by Jason Mankey

Ireland's Trees: Myths, Legends and Folklore by Niall MacCoitir

A Modern Herbal, Vol II by Margaret Grieve

New World Witchery: A Trove of North American Folk Magic by Cory Thomas Hutcheson

Popular Magic: Cunning-folk in English History by Owen Davies

The Robert Cochrane Letters: An Insight into Modern Traditional Witchcraft by Robert Cochrane with Evan John Jones

Tales of Galloway by Alan Temperley

Traditional Wicca: A Seeker's Guide by Thorn Mooney

Traditional Witchcraft: A Cornish Book of Ways by Gemma Gary

The Triumph of the Moon: A History of Modern Pagan Witchcraft by Ronald Hutton

The Witch: A History of Fear, from Ancient Times to the Present by Ronald Hutton

The Witch's Cabinet: Plant Lore, Sorcery and Folk Tradition by Corinne Boyer

Witches, Ghosts and Signs: Folklore of the Southern Appalachians by Patrick W. Gainer

Websites, Articles and Other Sources

http://www.bellwitch.org/story.htm

https://www.thenationalcouncil.org/wp-content/uploads/2022/08/Trauma-infographic.pdf

"An American Witch Bottle" by M.J. Becker, *Archaeology*, Vol. 33, No. 2 (March/April 1980), pp. 18–23 (https://www.jstor.org/stable/41726316)

"The Mandrake Fiend" by H. F. Clark, *Folklore*, Vol. 73, No. 4 (Winter, 1962), pp. 257–269

"The Pomander" by Rudolf Schmitz, *Pharmacy in History*, Vol. 31, No. 2 (1989), pp. 86–90, Published by: University of Wisconsin Press (https://www.jstor.org/stable/41112489)

"Traditional Uses and Folklore of Hypericum in the British Isles" by A.R. Vickery, *Economic Botany*, Vol. 35, No 3, published 1981 by Springer on behalf of New York Botanical Garden Press (https://www.jstor.org/stable/4254297)

"Witchcraft in North Carolina" by Tom Peete Cross, *Studies in Philology*, Vol. 16, No. 3 (Jul., 1919), pp. 217–287, Published by: University of North Carolina Press

Interview with John Welwood by Tina Fossella, first published in *Tricycle Magazine (https://tricycle.org/magazine/human-nature-buddha-nature/)*

Acknowledgments

An utmost expression of gratitude to the Witches, folklorists, educators, students, philosophers, healers, and curious minds whose work continues to inspire me every day. Your heart and work have inspired my own magical path and leading a life that resonates with my spirit. To my partner in life who has more confidence in me than anyone I've ever met and who supports every step I take: Where would I be without your pep talks? To my dearest friends who have witnessed my struggles as well as celebrated my achievements, you are truly sunshine on my cloudy days. To my ancestors who have been a guide and support along the way of walking a new path—this one is for you.

About the Author

LEAH MIDDLETON is a traditional Witch whose practice is inspired by her ancestral roots within Appalachia and beyond in regions within England and Scotland. She began sharing her practice with others in online spaces and learned that many resonated with it. With her first book, *The Beginner Witch's Handbook*, she paints a picture for the Witch at any level to create a practice that feels authentic to them by introducing ancestral lore and wisdom. Today, Leah continues to share her personal magical journey through her social channels at The Redheaded Witch.

INDEX

An ABC of Witchcraft, Past and Present (Valiente), 81
ABRACADABRA charm, 158–59
activities
  ancestor altar construction, 53
  call back energy, 75
  crafting ancestor connection incense blend, 53
  crafting family tree, 44
  incantation on mirrors, 21
  rite of passage, 17–18
  self-introduction to local spirits, 30–31
  spirit flight, 79
  summoning ancestor, 60–61
  taking safe root, 73–75
acts of service, 55
All Hallows' Eve, 47, 91, 110
ancestor altar creation, 51–53
ancestral lore and wisdom, 37
  addressing troubled ancestor, 68–69
  ancestor altar creation, 51–53
  beginning ancestral veneration, 54–62
  connecting to local community, 67
  crafting ancestor connection incense blend, 53
  discovering heritage, 46–50
  folk magic, 38–39
  forging new path, 63–67
  spiritual connection with magic, 38
  traditional witchcraft practices, 39
  uncovering roots, 40–46
ancestral trauma, 63–65
ancestral veneration, 54
  acts of service, 55
  ancestral spirit reflection, 62
  food and beverages offerings, 57
  gift-giving, 56–57
  learning ancestors' language, 58
  quality time, 56
  studies of folklore, 58–59
  summoning ancestor, 60–61
  visiting ancestors' homeland, 57–58
  words of affirmation, 55–56
Animism: Respecting the Living World (Harvey), 26
animism, 26
animistic Witch, 26–29

anointment oil. *See also* oil of Witch
  healing, 148
  for protection, 137–38
  walking in Witch's path, 152–53
apothecary, 85
  cabinet of Witch, 89–90
Appalachian Mountains
  belief of natural gateways to Otherworld, 32
  Bell Witch from, 13
  cornbread use in, 124
  deities in, 34–35
  folk beliefs of, 23
  horseshoe uses in Appalachian lore, 100
  practitioner of healing medicine, 15
  rite of passage, 10
  stories of spirits, 29
Ash plant, 134
attraction poppet bed, 106
autumnal equinox, 92

basil, 77, 89, 156, 157
Bay plant, 89, 101, 134, 137, 142
Bell, John, 13
Bell Witch, 13
besom, 76, 84, 122–23
Bill Against Conjurations, Enchantments, and Witchcrafts, 11
BIPOC community
  culture of, 46
  inability to access family records, 40
Book of Psalms, 81
bottle of Witch, 87, 130–31
Braveheart, Maria Yellow Horse, 65
broom. *See* besom

Calendar of Witch, 91–92
calendula, 89
candles of Witches, 85, 87, 138–39
Carmichael, Alexander, 158
cauldron, 16, 71, 81, 84, 101, 123, 154, 157
  brew, 109, 121
Celtic paganism, 23, 34
chamomile, 77, 89, 102–3
charm bags, 87
  healing illness, 158–59
  for protection, 132–33
  speak my truth, 156–57
charm(s), 21, 77
  spoken, 88
  for witchery, 11
  wreath, 134–35
Chiron, 154
Christianity, 23, 32–33
Christmas, 47

cinnamon, 89, 98, 105, 109, 121, 123
Clan of Tubal Cain practice, 24, 33
cleansing of Witch practices, 113. *See also* crafting magical practice; healing practice of Witches; protection of Witch practices
  cauldron brew, 121
  crafting besom, 122–23
  healing waters, 114–15
  home blessing cornbread, 124–25
  home reset floor wash, 118–19
  old self ritual, 126–27
  Witch's powder, 116–17
clock of Witch, 93
clothing, articles of, 51
Cochrane, Robert, 23–24, 33, 81
coffee, 49, 54, 89
Compass Rite, 81, 85
The Complete Herbal (Culpeper), 28
cord cutting candle
  lore, 96
  spell, 96–97
cornbread, home blessing
  lore, 124
  spell, 125
cornflower, 89, 107, 154
Cornish tradition, 134
Cornish Traditional Witchcraft (Gary), 23
crab apple tree, 109
crafting magical practice, 71. *See also* cleansing of Witch practices; healing practice of Witches; protection of Witch practices
  art of spellcrafting, 80–81
  gathering Witch's tools, 83–86
  grounding practice, 72
  incantation to call back energy, 75
  putting "craft" in witchcraft, 86–88
  sacred space creation, 82
  spirit flight, 76–79
  taking safe root, 73–75
  Witch's altar, 83
  Witch's apothecary cabinet, 89–90
  Witch's Calendar, 91–92
  Witch's clock, 93
craftsmanship, 55
crooked path of Witch, 15
Culpeper, Nicholas, 28

culture
    ancestral discovery through, 46–48
    of Otherworld, 32
cunning-folk, 11–13
cup, 85
cursing, 24, 25

Dark Moon, 93
deities, 32–33
dePaola, Tomie, 13
Devil
    associated with Witch, 34
    magic associated with, 10–11, 13
    Witch's pact with, 17
Devil's Nettle. See Yarrow (Achillea millefolium)
divination oil, 107
DNA discovery of ancestors, 41

enchanted ancestor charms
    lore, 140
    spell, 140–41

Faefolk, tale of, 58–59
family tree of ancestors, 40–43
    ancestor reflection, 46
    ancestor tree reflection, 45
    crafting, 44
fauna, 27, 47
Fitzhugh, Pat, 13
flora, 27
    self-introduction to, 30
    Witch's connection with, 28
    of Yarrow, 58
flying ointment, 76–77
folklore
    spirits of, 28–29
    studies of ancestors, 58–59
folk magic, 38–39
folk practices in New World, 118
folktales
    of place for grimoire, 31
    spirits conversation with, 27
food and beverages offerings, 57
forest, 15
Four Thieves Vinegar, 118
Full Moon, 93
    cord cutting candle spell at, 96
    divination practices at, 107
    rite of passage at, 18
    sharing with ancestor altar at, 68
    spirit flight at, 79

Gaelic incantation, 158
gamblers, 102
garden sage, 90
Gardner, Gerald, 7, 23, 24
garlic, 90, 135
Gary, Gemma, 23, 110
gift-giving, 56–57

Gladstar, Rosemary, 146
Gowdie, Isobel, 12
gratitude, 149, 152, 153
Gratitude Potion, 149
grief, 6, 40, 64, 66
Grimm Brothers, 12–13
Grimm, Gretel, 12–13
Grimm, Hänsel, 12–13
grimoire of Witch, 9, 24, 86. See also Witch
    ancestor culture reflection, 48
    ancestor reflection, 46
    ancestors within other communities reflection, 50
    ancestral spirit reflection, 62
    folktales of place for, 31
    Otherworld for, 35
    spells, 25
grounding practice, 72, 74

hag stone charm, 77
    lore, 142
    spell, 142–43
Harvey, Graham, 26
hawthorne, 90
hawthorn trees, 122, 150
healing practice of Witches, 63–64, 145. See also cleansing of Witch practices; crafting magical practice; protection of Witch practices
    anointing oil, 148
    bid my worries away spell, 154–55
    healing illness charm bag, 158–59
    healing waters, 114
    rooted in gratitude ritual, 149
    speak my truth charm bag, 156–57
    supporting physical and spiritual heart spell, 150–51
    traditional fire cider, 146–47
    walking in present ritual, 152–53
hedge-crossing. See spirit flight
herbal allies in spells, 89
heritage discovery of ancestors, 46
    ancestor culture reflection, 48
    ancestors within other communities, 49–50
    through culture, 46–48
hexing, 24, 25
historical trauma, 65
The History of Witches and Wizards, (W.P.), 78

home reset floor wash, cleansing by
    lore, 118
    spell, 118–19
Horned God, 34
horseshoe as tool to repel against Devil, 100, 101
Hutton, Ronald, 10

incantation
    to call back energy, 75
    on mirrors, 21
    to strengthen inner voice, 22–24
    writing, 88

Jenkins, James, 42
jewelry worn, 51
Juniper, 90, 121

knife, 84

lavender, 90
learning ancestors' language, 58
lemon balm, 90
LGBTQ+ community, ancestors within, 49
liminal space, 77–78
liquid offerings, 85
lore, 138
    basil, 156
    besom, 122
    cauldron brew, 121
    charm bags, 158
    of cord cutting candle, 96
    cornflower, 154
    of divination oil, 107
    of hag stones, 142
    hawthorn trees, 150
    healing waters, 114
    home blessing cornbread, 124
    home reset floor wash, 118
    of love thyself potion, 98
    motherwort, 148
    old self ritual cleansing, 126
    of opening new opportunities, 100
    prayers beads, 140
    of rest well sleep potion, 102
    rooted in gratitude ritual, 149
    SATOR Square charm, 138
    of strengthen friendship and connection potion, 109
    traditional fire cider, 146
    walking in Witch's path, 152
    of warding against nightmares, 132
    of warding against unwanted visitors, 134
    Witch's bottle protection, 130

of Witch's Ladder, 110–11
of Witch's personal poppet, 104
of Witch's powder, 116
about Yarrow, 137
love thyself potion
lore, 98
speaking kindly to yourself, 99
spell, 98–99

magic, 10, 80
associated with Devil, 10–11, 13
circle, 80–81
cunning-folk and, 11
folk magic, 38–39
practices by Witch, 8
witchcraft associated with, 16
The Malleus Maleficarum, 78
Mandrake root (Mandragora officinarum), 77
medicines for witchery, 11
meditation, 34, 62, 74–75, 76, 101
military herb. See Yarrow (Achillea millefolium)
mirrors
incantation for self-discovery, 21
for self-discovery, 19–20
Modern Traditional Witchcraft, 24
mortar, 85, 88, 106, 116, 154
motherwort, 148
mountain ash, 122
mugwort, 53, 77, 90, 107, 123

needlecrafting, 87
nettle, 90, 118–19
New Moon, 93
performing cauldron brew at, 121
spell for opening new opportunities on, 100–101
New World, 64
ancestral spirits in, 66
folk practices in, 118
nightmares, warding against
lore, 132
spell, 133
nightshades, 77

oak, 85, 122
oil of Witch, 88, 107. See also anointment oil
Old Ones, 32–35
old self ritual cleansing
lore, 126
spell, 126–27
opening new opportunities
lore, 100

spell, 100–101
Open Path Collective, 64
Otherworld, 6, 32
ancestral spirits as source of guidance and support in, 54
belief of, 32–35
conversations of, 7
experiences with, 9
for grimoire, 35
hag stone use in, 77
hawthorn trees relationship with, 150
liminal space use in, 77–78
magic circle, 80–81
mirrors as gateway to, 20
spirit flight, 76–79
Witch in, 76
oxymel, 146

passionflower, 77, 90, 106
pestle, 85, 88, 106, 116, 154
Phoebe Ward, 76
physical realm, 7, 11, 15, 21, 25, 54, 76, 78, 81, 104, 105, 111
pine, 53, 78, 122
poppet of Witch, 87
attraction poppet bed, 106
lore, 104
prosperity poppet bed, 105
spell, 104, 106
travel protection poppet bed, 106
potioncrafting, 88
powder of Witch, 88, 116–17
prayers beads, 140
prosperity poppet bed, 105
protection of Witch practices, 129. See also; cleansing of Witch practices; crafting magical practice; healing practice of Witches
anointing oil for, 137
enchanted ancestor charms, 140–41
hag stone charm, 142–43
of walls, 138–39
warding against nightmares, 132–33
warding against unwanted visitors, 134–35
Witch's bottle, 130–31

quality time, 31, 41, 56

rest well sleep potion, 102–3
rite(s), 8, 9, 32, 54, 71, 86
of passage, 17–18
performance by Witch, 10–11

ritual
addressing troubled ancestor, 68–69
ancestral, 78
call back energy, 75
magic circle, 81
rooted in gratitude, 149
spirit flight, 79
summoning ancestor, 60–61
veneration practice, 27, 56
walking in present, 152–53
witchcraft practice, 21
roots of ancestors, 40
ancestor tree reflection, 45
crafting family tree, 44
family tree, 40–43
lineage learning, 43
rose, 90, 98, 135
rosehips, 90
rosemary, 90
Rowan's Cross, 134
Rowan tree, 27–28, 122, 134

sacred space creation, 82
Samhain. See All Hallows' Eve
SATOR Square charm, 138–39
seasonal cycles, 92
self-exploration, 66
self-sabotage, 96
sigil crafting, 88
speak my truth charm bag, 156–57
spellcrafting, 80–81
spell doll, 87
spell(s), 21, 25, 159
anointing oil, 137, 148
besom, 122–23
bid my worries away, 154–55
cauldron brew, 121
of cord cutting candle, 96–97
for divination oil, 107
enchanted ancestor charms, 140–41
hag stone charm, 142–43
healing waters, 114–15
home blessing cornbread, 125
home reset floor wash, 118–19
of love thyself potion, 98–99
old self ritual cleansing, 126–27
for opening new opportunities, 100–101
for protection of walls, 138–39
for protection of Witch's bottle, 130, 131
for rest well sleep potion, 103
rooted in gratitude ritual, 149

speak my truth charm bag, 156–57
for strengthen friendship and connection potion, 109
supporting physical and spiritual heart spell, 150–51
traditional fire cider, 146–47
walking in present ritual, 152–53
for warding against nightmares, 133
for warding against unwanted visitors, 134–35
for Witch's Ladder, 110–11
for Witch's personal poppet, 104, 106
of Witch's powder, 116–17
spirit(s), 8, 15
connection with own spirit, 19–20
conversation with folktales, 27
experiences with, 9
fauna, 27
flight, 76–79
flora, 27
of folklore, 28–29
of place, 26
self-introduction to local spirits, 30–31
trees, 27
of water, 114
spirit of Witch, 95
cord cutting candle, 96–97
divination oil, 107
love thyself potion, 98–99
opening new opportunities, 100–101
rest well sleep potion, 102–3
strengthen friendship and connection potion, 108–9
Witch's Ladder, 110–11
Witch's personal poppet, 102–6
spiritual/spirituality
bypassing, 65–66
connection with ancestors, 51, 52, 54
conversations of, 7
Western spirituality movement, 74–75
spring equinox, 92
staff or stang tool, 85
star anise, 132
Starling, Mhara, 23
St. John's wort, 158, 159
Strega Nona (dePaola), 13
summer solstice, 92

supporting physical and spiritual heart spell, 150–51
symbols in crafting, 88

talismans, 77, 87, 131
thyme, 90, 146
traditional fire cider of Witch lore, 146
spell, 146–47
Traditional Witchcraft: A Cornish Book of Ways (Gary), 23
traditional witchcraft practice, 20, 23
of ancestors, 39
spirits of place, 26
Witch's ethics, 24–25
travel protection poppet bed, 106
trees/plant, 27–28, 80, 91, 93
Ash plant, 134
Bay plant, 89, 101, 134, 137, 142
crab apple tree, 109
family tree of ancestors, 40–43
hawthorn, 122, 150
Rowan tree, 27–28, 122, 134
trinkets, 16, 51, 86
Tylor, E. B., 26

unwanted visitors, warding against
lore, 134
spell, 134–35

valerian, 90, 133, 152
Valiente, Doreen, 81
verbal gratitude, 56
vervain, 90, 116, 126
visiting ancestors' homeland, 57–58

walking Witch's path
animistic Witch, 26–29
connection with own spirit, 19–20
incantation on mirrors, 21
incantation to strengthen inner voice, 22–24
Otherworld and Old Ones, 32–35
paving way, 15–16
rite of passage, 17–18
self-introduction to local spirits, 30–31
traditional witchcraft practice, 20
Witch's ethics, 24–25
Walpurgis Night, 78
Waning Moon, 93
wassailing, 109
Waxing Moon, 93
Weeping Willow, 27–28

Welsh Witchcraft: A Guide to the Spirits, Lore, and Magic of Wales (Starling), 23
Welwood, John, 65
Western spirituality movement, 74–75
Wiccan Rede, 24
Wicca practice, 7–8, 23–24, 33
willow, 122
winter solstice, 47, 92
Witch, 8, 161
altar, 83
animistic, 26–29
apothecary cabinet, 89–90
bottle of, 87
bottle protection, 130–31
Calendar, 91–92
cleansing by Witch's powder, 116–17
clock, 93
vs. cunning-folk, 12
definition of, 10–11
Devil associated with, 34
ethics, 24–25
gathering tools, 83–86
haunting of, 13
home, 16
Ladder, 110–11
oil of, 88
personal poppet, 104–6
powder of, 88
traditional fire cider of, 146–47
trials, 24
witch trials, 12
Witchcraft Act (1735), 23
witchcraft practice, 7–8, 32, 71, 161
associated with magic, 16
putting "craft" in, 86–88
traditional practice, 20
Witchcraft Today (Gardner), 23
witchery, 6, 7, 10–11, 38
kitchen, 83, 84
in North America, 130
use of candles against, 85
use of horseshoe against, 100
Witch Father, 33
Witch Mother, 33
"the witch of Kate Batts," 13
Witch's tree. See hawthorn trees
words of affirmation, 55–56
W.P., 78

Yarrow (Achillea millefolium), 58, 90, 137, 159